IN
SEARCH
OF
MELANCHOLY
BABY

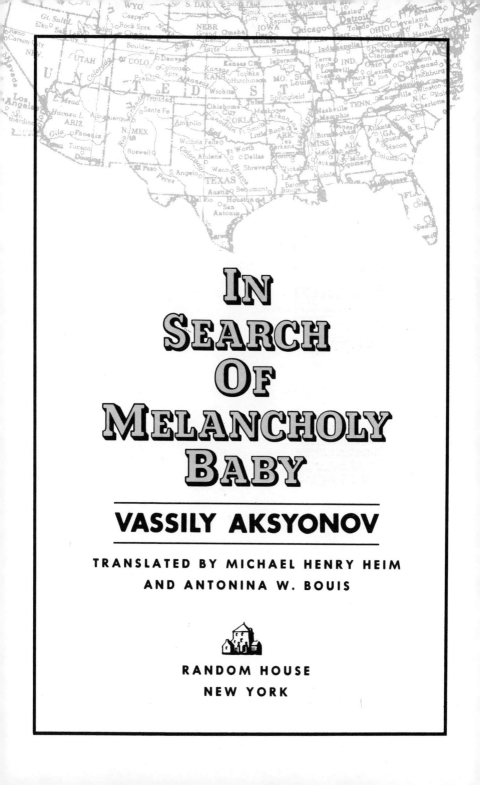

In Search Of Melancholy Baby

VASSILY AKSYONOV

TRANSLATED BY MICHAEL HENRY HEIM
AND ANTONINA W. BOUIS

RANDOM HOUSE
NEW YORK

Library of Congress Cataloging-in-Publication Data

Aksenov, Vasiliĭ Pavlovich, 1932-
    In search of melancholy baby.

    1. Akesenov, Vasiliĭ Pavlovich, 1932—Biography.
    2. Authors, Russian—20th century—Biography.
    3. Authors, Russian—United States—Biography.
    I. Title.
PG3478.K7Z465   1987   891.73'44 [B]   86-26211
ISBN 0-394-54364-5

Manufactured in the United States of America
24689753
First Edition

PREFACE

In Search of Melancholy Baby is the story of my emigration, alienation, and gradual acceptance of a new home.

It is actually my second book about America. The first, *Non-Stop Round the Clock,* was published by the Moscow journal *Novy Mir* after a trip I made through the United States in 1975 and might be compared to a stack of snapshots taken in haste through a rose-tinted lens.

Now I look at American life from a professional point of view—that is, as a novelist. One of my American dreams is the American novel, and that is why in the spaces between the chapters of nonfiction the reader will find "Sketches for a Novel to Be." These may be considered commercial messages.

IN SEARCH OF MELANCHOLY BABY

1 "Don't tell me you really mean to live in America!" said Klaus-Gabriel von Diederhofen, whose real name doesn't sound so impressive.

"And why not?" I asked.

He shrugged his shoulders.

"Klaus doesn't like America," said Sergio Bugaretti (another champagne name) with a wink. "You know why?"

Just then the director clapped his hands and told us to get ready for the camera, and each panelist assumed his own version of dignity: the German perching a pair of wire-rimmed glasses on his short nose to look more proletarian; the Italian tossing his gray locks back from his forehead to establish closer contact with the audience; the Russian émigré—which is to say a forty-eight-year-old writer recently booted out of Moscow or, to be even more precise, yours truly—affecting serenity, sociability, and a worldly sheen, none of which was wholly in keeping with his situation at the moment.

We were sitting in directors' chairs at the peak of an ideally round, ideally green mountain. Beneath us, in the folds of the foothills, the brightly painted houses of a town whose name had the ring of a flute—Cortina d'Ampezzo; above us, all combs, towers, and fangs, the glacierlike slopes of the Dolomites.

In that summer of 1980 I was a celebrity in Italy. Several months before I left the Soviet Union, my novel *The Burn* had come out in Italian. Just after I left, some Italian journalists traced me to Paris, and the municipality of Cortina invited my wife and me to their blissful surroundings for a rest. There they had inveigled me onto a TV panel with their famous Bugaretti and his famous colleague from Hamburg. The whole thing would have smacked of a Cortina promotion spot if not for our less than youthful faces and the sour expressions that soon crept over them. Clearly the German didn't care for what I was saying; nor was I particularly happy with what *he* had to say; the Italian cared only for the mother tongue. I couldn't help thinking we were merely polluting the atmosphere, all three of us.

When the taping was over, we went to cool off in a little *trattoria*. Von Diederhofen brought up America again. Why leave Russia for America, one hell for another? Can't you see? Bugaretti smiled: The reason he hates America is that it refutes his beloved Spengler; it refuses to decline politely.

My head was still spinning from our last weeks in Moscow, when group after group of our old friends—and KGB informers—dropped in to say good-bye. Emigrating is something like going to your own funeral, the only difference being that after your funeral your nervous system calms down.

What has he got against America, that bigwig German? After all, I'd been there myself some five years earlier. What a blast! *Non-Stop Round the Clock* seemed the perfect name for the fanciful little travelogue I'd written afterward. At home you'd tune in the Voice of America for half an hour twice a day and all you got was static and wailing. No, there was no comparison.

"It's Germans like him who make you think Europe wouldn't have been much better off if Communist Thälmann had beat Nazi Hitler in the fateful elections back in the thirties."

"Well, his Italian crony is no great shakes either. You couldn't see his neck for the gold chains. Or his wrists. He's got the aesthetics of a Gabriele d'Annunzio and the mystique of neo-Roman decadence. What was that he said about Spengler?"

"Heaven only knows. To tell the truth, I can't quite remember who Spengler is."

The way my wife and I dealt with the indifference our companions had shown us was to ooze indifference to them. We were wrong, of course. The German was no Communist, the Italian no Fascist; both were merely respectable sinners, philosophical slobs, and chronic victims of the male menopause—in other words, Great European Writers. And as the darlings of Europe they didn't give a hoot about America and our projected journey there.

A TRAMPLED BUTTERFLY

We flew. For some reason nothing seemed quite up to snuff. The meal was synthetic, the movie pitiful, and the stewardesses tired and unsociable—very much like their Soviet, old-gray-mare counterparts. What was going on? Five years before I had flown across the very same ocean on the very same transworld airline and everything was just the reverse: top-notch food, sexy staff, Oscar-quality film . . .

I recalled a Ray Bradbury story about a guided tour to the prehistoric past. The tourists were warned that by straying so much as a step from their artificial path they might endanger the environment of the past and thereby cause unforeseen consequences in the future, that is, the time from which they had come and to which they intended to return. The hero of the story fails to watch where he is going and steps on a butterfly that has alighted on the edge of the path. So what, he thinks. Nothing's going to change on account of a butterfly that lived a million years ago. When he arrives back in his own era, he finds that nothing has in fact changed—except that an electoral campaign which had promised a victory for sanity and reason has taken an inexplicably irrational turn and the language of the media has grown semiliterate and coarse, and is full of vague threats.

The image of the trampled butterfly had not left me, I now realized, since the day I had set foot in the West, a new émigré. It had accompanied me through three months of wandering across Europe and was with me now on my flight to America. Everything had seemed better before, bigger, nicer; everything had seemed more sensible and less smelly: less sweat *and* less deodorant.

Maybe the deterioration was only a figment of my imagination; maybe things always seem to deteriorate; maybe the misanthropic miasmas heralded the onset of my own midlife crisis. Though perhaps the impudent oil embargo of 1973 had proved to be a "trampled butterfly" for Western civilization, and its aftereffects were lingering on in the guise of minor, all but invisible setbacks which, taken together, gave off a stench of hackwork and toppling standards.

The pithiest travel description I have ever read occurs in a Russian novel dating from the late eighteenth century. The novel is entitled *The Adventures of a Smithy Bridge Milliner and a Carriage Row Chambermaid,* and it comes burdened with nothing extraneous, not even its author's name. The entire description reads as follows: "Now on to Sokolniki, and here we are in Sokolniki!"

So on to America, and here we are in America!

Brevity of this ilk is unfortunately as lost upon contemporary airports as upon contemporary writers. At JFK we faced endless lines at passport control, a crush at the baggage carousels, and swarms from each of all possible worlds (with an emphasis on the third) at customs. Still— Klaus-Gabriel von Diederhofen, take note—the border illustrates a cardinal difference between the USSR and the USA: the former gruffly bars its people's way across the motherland's "sacred boundaries" while the latter rather lackadaisically fends off those trying to push their way under its star-spangled shelter. And of course, if you feel like leaving, go right ahead!

HATING THE STATES

Even now, after living in America for more than five years, I keep wondering what provokes so many people in Latin America, Russia, and Europe to anti-American sentiment of such intensity that it can only be called hatred. There is something oddly hysterical about it all, as if America were not a country but a woman who has hurt a man's pride by cheating on him.

Let us forget (for the time being) the role of anti-American propaganda in the strategy of the opposition, which, in the case of the Soviet Union, is managed by the anything but friendly people down at Agitprop. In the international arena this "war of ideas" exists on a par with bacteriological warfare and the anthrax bomb. Let us limit our discussion to feelings, complexes, and unconscious hostility.

A Soviet poet once asked the revolutionary Ernesto "Che" Guevara why he hated America with such a passion, and Che launched into a tirade against Yankee imperialism, the enslavement of economically underdeveloped nations by rapacious monopolies, expansionism, the suppression of national liberation movements, and so on. The poet, to give him his due, found Che's lesson in political literacy less than satisfactory and inquired whether there wasn't perhaps something personal behind his feelings. After a few moments of silence, during which the ever-present daiquiri turned slowly in his fingers, Che cast a glance in the direction of Florida (let us imagine the conversation taking place on board the *Granma*) and launched into a curious story. Since I'm not sure the story has made it into the biographies adorning leftist bookshop windows these days, I will retell it as I heard it from the poet.

As a teenager in Argentina, Ernesto made a cult of the

United States. He was wild about Hollywood westerns and the latest jazz. One day, riding his bike past the airport, he saw a plane being loaded with racehorses for America. Instantly the revolutionary in him took over. Think of it—a free ride to the land of virile cowboys and forward blondes. All he had to do was stow away. No sooner said than done: on to America, and here he is in America.

In Georgia to be exact. A hundred degrees in the shade. When the ground crew discovered the Argentine adventurer, they beat him black and blue and locked him back up in the empty plane. For three days they left him there to bake without food or water. Then they sent him home.

"I'll never forgive them that airplane," Che whispered to the poet. And flaring up again: "I hate all gringos, their easygoing voices, insolent struts, confident leers, obscene smiles . . ."

Other Latin American anti-American revolutionaries— the Sandinistas in Nicaragua, for instance—may have just such a "plane" in their backgrounds. And even if it was not quite so burning an issue as Che made of it, even if it was incidental and short-lived, it was still a blow to their self-esteem, a humiliating slap in the face. How to deal with it? Blame the fair-haired colossus of the North. Provincial inferiority complexes have played an enormous part in the spread of Marxist doctrine.

Simplistic as it may sound, many if not most of these "planes" can be chalked up to misunderstandings. Americans take no pleasure in humiliating people. Their "pushy voices" reflect the intonation patterns of American speech, their "insolent struts" the way generations of American bodies have learned to propel themselves from one place to another. As for "confident leers" and "obscene smiles," they are not commonly found among the populace, and when they do occur they generally represent an innocent attempt to copy the latest TV or movie look. Besides, the image of the American superman is quickly becoming a thing of the past. Take the sad and instructive case of the

American marines entrenched on the outskirts of Beirut in 1983. Soviet propaganda raised an international hue and cry about American invaders and rapists, but if you had taken a good look at them you would have seen they were just a bunch of kids, young working-class kids. The "insolent struts," "obscene smiles," and "confident leers" belonged to the more-American-than-the-Americans Arab terrorists roaming the streets of the devastated city and surrounding hills. Anti-American sentiment is essentially hatred for an outdated stereotype, a celluloid phantom.

It would be interesting to trace the roots of anti-American feelings in societies where ideology reigns supreme. Goebbels could not get over the interrogations of the first American prisoners of war (they were captured in the Sahara). They have no ideology, *mein Führer,* he announced. In other words, they lacked all human qualities.

I believe it is the same lack of ideology that so infuriates today's West German leftists. When a leader of the Greens filled a test tube with his own blood and splashed it over the uniform of an American general, I was reminded of the Nazi spirit in its early days.

On the other hand, I am certain that despite decades of propaganda the Russians have not yet developed an anti-American complex. True, the post-Revolutionary Russian intelligentsia, itself a part of the European left, has mistrusted (or is it now "used to mistrust"?) American civilization in the abstract, but perhaps my Italian friend Bugaretti was not so far from the truth when he invoked Spengler: America does in fact refute Spengler's thesis of the decline of the West.

The first Russian revolutionary writer to visit the United States was Maksim Gorky; the year was 1906. The "stormy petrel of revolution" was terribly irritated by the place. He labeled New York "the city of the Yellow Devil" and called jazz, with the total lack of aesthetic sensibility that was his trademark, "the music of the fat."

In 1931 Boris Pilnyak, one of the great prose stylists of

the previous decade, visited the States and wrote an "American novel" entitled *Okay*. Unfortunately, another four-letter word would have described it better. Pilnyak's anti-Americanism must have been the envy of many an Agitprop hack. At every crossroads he would beat his breast and proclaim with the utmost vulgarity, "I am a Soviet man!" Everything disgusted him. He fled in panic from a vaudeville chorus line: "How can a Soviet writer show his face before such bare-bellied floozies?" And this from a man who had fought to bring naturalism and sex to puritanical Russian literature. There is always the chance that Pilnyak used *Okay* to make amends to Stalin for his ambiguous "Tale of the Unextinguished Moon" or that he was bitter about a short-lived movie contract he was given in Hollywood, but I discern a modicum of sincerity behind it all.

The poet Vladimir Mayakovsky was torn between delight and hostility during his stay in America a few years earlier. The futurist, artistic side of him reveled in the skyscrapers and enormous steel bridges, and Broadway's Great White Way got his creative juices going. But the leftist, the revolutionary, the Trotskyite in him pushed in a different direction. Here is a literal version of one of his "American" poems:

> *I'm wild about New York City,*
> *Though I'm not about to bow to you.*
> *We Soviets have our own pride*
> *And look down at the bourgeoise*
> *With our noses in the air.*

In his prophetic way Mayakovsky saw that the United States would become the last bastion of capitalism. He was seconded in this view and in his general feelings for the country by the satirists Ilf and Petrov in their 1936 travelogue, *One-Story America*.

As I see it, all these Russian (read: leftist European)

literary travelers were crushed by America's total indifference to the cardinal event of their lives, the October Revolution. Some, like Mayakovsky, were able to accept the revolution lock, stock, and barrel; others, like Pilnyak, were more ambivalent. But for the European left as a whole it meant a New Flood, a great cleansing process, the birth pangs of a new society.

Everything seemed to come into focus after the revolution. All the predictions about the decline of Europe and the demise of Western civilization had apparently come true. Even the reactionary governments of England and France could feel the new age dawning. Oppose it as they might, the sun had risen in the East. Many of us may grieve in our hearts for the world we have lost, for its elegance and manners and horn of plenty, yet we still fall in step with the thunderous march of the class now on the offensive, we still add our voices to the symphony of the future. . . . And suddenly we learn that on the other side of the ocean there is a gigantic society that does not quite grasp the oratory of the New Flood prophets and looks upon our great cosmic event, our revolution, as a tempest in a samovar. This society, the United States of North America, scandalously refuses to pay attention to Marx or Spengler or Lenin. It shows no intention of disappearing or disintegrating or sinking into decadence. It has no time. It turns its frenzied energy to making money, money, money, a squalid, unseemly proposition resulting in skyscrapers the likes of which the Old World has never imagined and a network of highways crisscrossing the nation. Instead of making revolutions, the workers are buying cars!

Pilnyak, Mayakovsky, and Ilf and Petrov—they all sensed deep down that America represented an alternative to violent revolution. How could they help feeling threatened? America had called into question the great cause to which they had lent their lives.

Now, in the twilight of the Communist world, the threat is all the greater. Many Soviet leaders cannot help realizing that the world they represent is no "new world" at all but a world long past its prime. From today's vantage point the Russian Revolution looks like nothing so much as an outmoded and absurd act of violence, the kind of thing one would expect from a society in the early stages of European bourgeois decadence. American capitalism, on the other hand—riding the crest of a completely different revolution, the technological one—is on its way to a truly new, as yet unknown and undefined age of liberalism.

LOVING THE STATES

In 1952, when I was a nineteen-year-old student from the provinces, I found myself thrust into Moscow's high society. I had been invited to a party at the house of an important diplomat. The guests consisted mainly of diplomatic corps brats and their girlfriends. It was the first time I had ever seen an American radiola, the kind that let you stack twelve records at a time. And what records! Back in Kazan we spent hours fiddling with the dials on our bulky wireless receivers for even a snatch of jazz and here it was in all its glory—with the musicians' pictures on the albums to boot. There they all were: Bing Crosby, Nat King Cole, Louis Armstrong, Peggy Lee, Woody Herman . . .

One girl I danced with asked me the most terrifying question: "Don't you just love the States?"

I mumbled something vague. How could I openly admit to loving America when from just about every issue of *Pravda* or *Izvestia* Uncle Sam bared his ugly teeth at us and stretched out his long, skinny fingers (drenched in the blood of the freedom-loving peoples of the world) for new victims. Overnight our World War II ally had turned back into our worst enemy.

"Well, I do!" she said, lifting her doll-like face in a challenge as I concentrated on twirling her correctly. "I hate the Soviet Union and adore America!"

Such trepidation shocked me speechless, and the girl dropped me on the spot: The provincial drip! Was he out of it!

Sulking in a corner, I scrutinized the mysterious young beauties gliding across the darkened room—the shiny hair so neatly parted, the suave, white-toothed smiles, the Camels and Pall Malls, the sophisticated English vocabulary ("darling," "baby," "let's drink")—and their partners, so elegantly attired in jackets with huge padded shoulders, tight black trousers, and thick-soled shoes. Our gang in Kazan did everything it could to ape American fashion; our girls knit us sweaters with deer on them and embroidered our ties with cowboys and cactuses. But it was only imitation, do-it-yourself. This was the genuine article, made in the USA.

"Wow, what class!" I gushed to the friend who'd wangled me the invitation. But when I referred to the crowd as "real *stilyagi*" (the name given to the disaffected, Western-looking Soviet youth of the fifties), he corrected me arrogantly—though he himself fit in only slightly better than I—saying, "We're not *stilyagi;* we're Stateniks!"

As I subsequently discovered, there were whole pockets of America lovers in Moscow, and all of them rejected even French fashion in favor of American. Wearing a shirt with buttons that had two or three holes instead of the requisite American four, for example, was considered a disgrace. "Hey, man," your Statenik pals would say, "there's something wrong with your getup."

(I might add that I have met more than one Statenik-turned-émigré who has rejected everything stateside, drives a Volkswagen, and wears the latest in Italian fashion.)

The party I went to climaxed in a spectacular boogie-woogie with the girls flying this way and that. I looked on transfixed as the skirt of my former partner sailed up toward the ceiling. It was all so real—not only the dance but the skirt and what I'd glimpsed under it. I later found out she was the daughter of a high-ranking KGB officer.

Who in the States would have thought that at the height of the cold war, America had such devoted allies among the Soviet elite? Recently a German director and I were throwing some ideas for a film satire back and forth. The setting is a large European hotel, where a round of Soviet-American disarmament talks has been going on for several months. We see the heads of the negotiation teams, both men in their fifties, sitting face to face. "They don't understand each other, of course," the director said. "They're from different backgrounds, different worlds." "Not so," I objected. "They both may have jitterbugged to Elvis a few years back."

Among the Soviet rank and file, pro-American feeling had a more material base: the people connected the word "America" with the miracle of tasty and nourishing foodstuffs in the midst of wartime misery. Bags of yellow egg powder and containers of condensed milk and cured ham saved hundreds of thousands of Soviet children from starving to death. American Studebakers and Dodges were instrumental in keeping lines of communication open throughout the war. Without them the Soviet Army would have taken not two but ten years to advance. America provided a lifeline during a period of total death—and what a life that line led to: it was like nothing we Soviets could even imagine. The American presence gave the ordinary Soviet citizen a vague hope for change after the war was over.

Before the war that ordinary citizen had little sense of America. True, the country figured in a few crude ditties, but they reflect more the offbeat surrealism of folk humor than anything else. A typical example:

America gave Russia a steam-driven boat.
It had two giant wheels but barely stayed afloat.

Or even worse:

> *An American—alas!—*
> *Stuck a finger up his ass*
> *And thought—what a laugh!—*
> *He'd wound up his phonograph.*

Despite the almost total absence of a Russian "sense of America," both these masterpieces relate in their own way to technology. America has always been connected with something revolving and springy.

Not until the war did Russians acquire a firm sense of America as a country of fabled riches and munificence. The brief, euphoric period of postwar contact in Europe gave rise to the opinion that Russians and Americans were in fact very much alike. When you tried to pin Russians down about what it was that made the two peoples so similar, they tended to say something like: "Americans are down to earth and enjoy a drink." "And do they like to raise Cain?" you might ask to pin them down even further. "No, they don't" would be the reply, "but they can kick up a hell of a rumpus when they feel like it."

The decades of anti-American propaganda that followed have done little to shake this belief. Strange as it may seem, the Russians still think of Americans as close relations. The Chinese, on the other hand, they think of as beings from outer space. And although the idea of communism traveled to China via Russia, the Russian in his heart of hearts believes that if anyone is predisposed toward communism it is the Chinese, not he or his fellow Russians.

In 1969, during the skirmishes along the Sino-Soviet border, I happened to be in nearby Alma-Ata, the capital of Soviet Kazakhstan. One day I shared a table at the hotel restaurant with an officer from the local missile base. Before long he was dead drunk and weeping like a child: "There's a war about to break, and I've just bought a motorcycle, a real beaut, a Jawa. It took me five long years to save up, and now the Chinese'll come and grab it." "So you're scared of the Chinese?" I said. "Not in the least," he slobbered. "I just don't want to lose my motorcycle." At this point I couldn't help putting a rather provocative question to him, namely, "What about the Americans, Lieutenant? Are you scared of them?" Whereupon he sobered up for a moment and said in a firm voice, "Americans respect private property."

The official goal of Soviet society is to reach the stage of historical development known as communism. For want of religious underpinning, the goal has taken on a purely pragmatic and rather feebleminded "self-help" kind of image; it is now a means of "satisfying the ever-growing demands of the working people." In 1960 Khrushchev set out to overtake America (Soviet production statistics have always been measured against American production statistics) and build a Communist (that is, in the popular imagination, prosperous) society, both by 1980. Although the Soviet Union might have overtaken America in the production of tanks, it failed everywhere else: the bounty of Safeway shelves still surpasses the wildest dreams of the Soviet consumer, plagued now as then by never-ending lines and shortages. As for communism, it still seems to be receding into the future.

The combination of vague pro-American feelings and an all-out anti-American propaganda campaign caused a certain segment of Soviet society to start leaning unconsciously in the direction of America in matters aesthetic, emotional, and even to some extent ideological. I have in mind the Soviet intelligentsia of my generation.

It is no easy task to explain the exodus from the Soviet orbit of a generation so thoroughly ready for Soviet life. (What could have been better preparation than the arrests of our fathers during the 1937 purges?) Theoretically, we ought to have turned into "new men" even more ideal than our elder brothers, the intellectuals who went off *as volunteers* to fight against Finland in the belief that their infamous sally would further the great revolutionary struggle for liberation. As far as they were concerned, everything emanating from the Kremlin had a noble, radiant aura. Members of the celebrated Institute of Philosophy and Literature condoned both the purges of the thirties and the anticosmopolitan campaign of the forties. For these intellectuals, many of whom spent time in the camps for their Communist ardor, the unmasking of Stalin was a catastrophe, the "thaw" an excruciating process of self-reevaluation.

For us, however, it was the start of a great carnival. Down with Stalin! Up with jazz! We were ready for the about-face; in fact, we had been ready since before Stalin's death. Far behind the indestructible iron curtain we had somehow managed to develop a pro-Western mentality—and what could be farther west than America?

A number of films, gleaned from the booty brought back from Germany after the war, fell into the hands of the authorities. Most were sentimental trash or Nazi-made anti-British products, but here and there an American classic of the thirties would turn up. The authorities, looking for a way to bring in money, decided to swallow their ideological pride and release them for public consumption. This decision, unusual enough in itself, was rendered even more so by the fact that the impossible burden of making ideologically pure pictures had forced the Soviet film industry to curb its output to three or four films a year.

Since the authorities had no intention of paying royalties on the films, they showed them under false titles. *Stagecoach,* for example, was called *The Journey Will Be Dangerous; Mr. Deeds Goes to Washington—The Dollar Rules; The Roaring Twenties—The Fate of a Soldier in America.* In addition to ideologically emended titles, the films received ludicrous introductions—"*The Journey Will Be Dangerous* treats the heroic struggle of the Indians against Yankee imperialism"—which replaced the credits and therefore prevented us from getting to know names like John Wayne and James Cagney.

I saw *Stagecoach* no fewer than ten times and *The Roaring*

Twenties no fewer than fifteen. There was a period when we spoke to our friends almost entirely in quotes from American movies. One such friend, after becoming a high-ranking officer in the Soviet Air Force, confided in me, "Comrade Stalin made a big mistake by letting our generation see those films." My friend was right: they provided one of the few windows to the outside world from our stinking Stalinist lair.

Another of those windows was provided by jazz. From the moment I heard a recording of "Melancholy Baby"—a pirate job on an X-ray plate—I couldn't get enough of the revelation coming to me through the shadows of ribs and alveoli, namely, that "every cloud must have a silver lining."

In those days jazz was America's secret weapon number one. Every night the Voice of America would beam a two-hour jazz program at the Soviet Union from Tangiers. The snatches of music and bits of information made for a kind of golden glow over the horizon when the sun went down, that is, in the West, the inaccessible but oh so desirable West. How many dreamy Russian boys came to puberty to the strains of Ellington's "Take the A Train" and the dulcet voice of Willis Conover, the VOA's Mr. Jazz. We taped the music on antediluvian recorders and played it over and over at semiunderground parties, which often ended in fistfights with Komsomol patrols or even police raids.

Clothes provided yet another window on the West. That is why, as I've pointed out, they turned into such a fetish. If a girl in an American dress (how did she come by it?) showed up walking along Leningrad's Nevsky Prospect, she would soon be followed by a crowd of *stilyagi*. Swinging and swaying (which is how they thought Americans moved along Broadway—they even nicknamed Nevsky Propsect "Broad"), they would sing, "I've met a girl/As sweet as can be/ Her name is Peggy Lee." The first satirical article about the *stilyagi* described a gang of youths swaggering down Nevsky Prospect in stars-and-stripes ties. When you think about it, *stilyagi* were the first dissidents.

Leningrad was far ahead of the rest of the country in terms of Westernization. Soon a Leningrad variety of know-it-all began to proliferate, a cat who could fill you in on anything and everything to do with America, from the early popular and later banned editions of Dos Passos and Hemingway in Russian to Dizzy Gillespie's latest Greenwich Village concert, (Last Saturday at the Half Note—no, sorry, man, it was Friday; Saturday was Charlie Parker, and was it pouring! Can't you just picture it, man? The rain, the Village—it's enough to make you piss your pants.)

The picture of America that our generation pieced together in its imagination was impossibly idealized and distorted, but it also had an amazing—astral, if you like—truth to it. No one paid much attention to the pro-American phenomenon at the time, but looking back on it now from a distance of thirty years I can say—without any pretense at scholarly analysis, of course—that the America cult had its roots in our basic antirevolutionary character. Not that we were aware of it at first. But what had once been called the "romance of the revolution" had all but evaporated by the time our generation came along; what is more, it had started giving way to a "romance of counterrevolution": the young now found the figure of the White Army officer more romantic than his Red counterpart. Unlike Gorky, Pilnyak, or Mayakovsky we refused—unconsciously as yet—to see the revolution as a latter-day deluge, a force of universal purification. We knew that instead of purity it had brought in its wake the monstrously bloody, monstrously dreary Stalinist way of life.

America rose up out of the mist as an alternative to an outdated and nauseating belief in Socialist revolution, that is, the revolt of the slaves against their masters. The intervening thirty years have dispelled many of my illusions, but on this point I have not wavered. In fact, I perceive with greater clarity that totalitarian decadence must be (and is now in the process of being) outweighed by the forces of liberalism and benevolent inequality. And I thank God that the leader of those forces is a powerful America.

Sketches for a Novel to Be

How does a novel come to its author? No one has written on the subject with more simplicity and grace than Pushkin:

> The outline of my freeborn novel? I'll peer into my magic ball. No, I can't make it out at all.

The outline of my American novel, flattened and elongated as if by a wide-angle lens, differs from the curious point (onto which it is projected) in superurbanized America, where Beethoven Street, alone and mysteriously named amid the grid of its numbered comrades, ducks under the concrete filigree of a freeway exit and comes to an abrupt halt in the form of a parking lot, an asphalt puddle above the dazzling expanse of either the Pacific or the Atlantic Ocean, where a couple of palms (or is it three?) . . . where three or four palms rattle their fronds in the wind . . . though the palms may turn out to be superfluous . . . . Be that as it may, my novel's hero now stands at one end of the parking lot and . . . who is he anyway?

The Hero of My Novel, HMN, Her Majesty's Navy . . .

Out of the blue a song from another era comes wafting past, and with it the title of my novel to be—*Melancholy Baby*.

Must every cloud have a silver lining?

And suddenly the melody wafts us back into our own past, our "Kazan orphan" period, the Volga, and Stalin . . .

1952/ Everyone called the girls at the language school "future spies." What's the point of studying a language if not to spy on the country where it's spoken?

A bevy of girls waiting in front of the Fur Workers Club box office (which continually reeked of urine—the local hooligans used one corner as a pissoir) for tickets to that evening's "booty movie," *The Fate of a Soldier in America.* Future spies all, from the minuscule local contingent of "good families." Thirty years later a lively black-eyed girl from the group came up to me in Brighton Beach's Black Sea bookshop and said, "You know what the real name of that movie was? *The Roaring Twenties.*"

Come to me, my melancholy baby. About fantasy, about bread, about love . . . (Sorry, but that was a bit later, in 1955, a song from a different opera, as we Russians say to mean a horse of a different color.) Every cloud must have a silver lining.

But *does* every cloud have a silver lining?

1980/ The condominium Pacifist Palisades, where the HMN was subletting a studio apartment for three hundred a month.

When his neighbor, the experienced American Gagik Sarkisian, saw him counting a roll of twenties, tips from his new job at Colonial Parking, he said to the HMN thoughtfully, "If I were you, I'd hand that money over to your experienced American neighbor to invest in his up-and-coming candied fruit business. Dentists or no dentists, the public will always have a sweet tooth."

The HMN thought awhile and replied, "I agree, and so I think I'll spend it on a Hawaiian weekend."

"Not a bad choice. Feel rich. It's one of America's greatest lessons."

1 9 5 6 / Strong point of the Vasilyev Island Komsomol Patrol. "Just you wait, you bastard. We'll cure you of your American dances. We'll cure you of your Polish revisionism! When we get done with you, you'll think you've been to the Wild West via Warsaw! What kind of Red Navy man are you, anyway? Just you wait. You'll love your country when we get through with you!"

2 "New York is like a snazzy broad who fusses with her hair but forgets to wipe her ass." Such was the view of the Russian musician who showed us the city during our first week in America. "And unfortunately, we émigrés inhabit her nether regions."

"Surely a bit of art-for-art's-sake overstatement on your part, eh Vova?"

"More like art-for-art's-sake understatement, I'm afraid. Feast your eyes on the skyline—fantastic, isn't it? Now look down at the street. All bumps, pits, and puddles. Add a couple of pigs and you've got a village as rude as Gogol's Ukrainian backwater. And you don't need to look far for pigs, either. Take that gentleman over there. A model swine, don't you think?"

One of the strongest impressions in that first week. Scene: Madison Avenue, a place where svelte, six-foot models alighting from limousines are as common as long queues of squat old crones armed with net shopping bags in Moscow. A pasty-faced gentleman steps up to a large cracked pot with a withering flower in it, undoes his fly, hauls out his equipment, does his business, tucks his equipment back in, and totters merrily on his way.

"Hm. See what you mean, Vova . . ."

"And doesn't a taxi ride down Seventh bring back the mud paths of Ryazan you wrote about in *Surplussed Barrelware*?" Though in Ryazan you didn't have to put up with noxious fumes. And those steam clouds of unknown provenance rising up from cracks in the asphalt a few feet from Tiffany's jewels. [People tell me they're New York's genies signaling back and forth.] And the filth! Not even Fifth Avenue can be hosed down to decency, and you don't see anybody taking a scrub brush to it.

"Then why do you live here, Vova? You've been all over since you emigrated—Paris, Jerusalem, London, Berlin, Rome. Why here?"

"Because New York's the only place you *can* live," said our fastidious friend. "Why do you think I went to all those places? To make sure I'd come to the right one. Now I know: New York is it." He paused a second and added, "New York or Moscow." And then, after another pause: "Though there's no going back . . ."

Vova rents an enormous SoHo loft in a building with a badly buckled façade. He picked out the street, besooted by what would seem a sempiternal blaze, and the building, a monster of late-nineteenth-century commercial architecture, before SoHo was SoHo, and pays an accordingly low rent. The stove is flanked by a grand piano. The bed, a two-minute walk away, consists of a pair of inflatable mattresses in a tent pitched beneath a patch of water-stained wall and a poster for *The Taming of the Shrew.*

New York has become the Mecca for a large part of the artistically inclined members of the new emigration—from its masters and craftsmen on down to the raggle-taggle bohemian fringe. Their New York existence differs little from their existence in Moscow or Peter (a popular pet name for Leningrad and a nostalgic leftover from its Petersburg days), except of course that they no longer need to start roaming the streets for beer the moment they get out of bed. When night falls, they still move like nomads from flat to flat, studio to studio, basement to attic, though the last is now more likely to be a loft or even a penthouse.

"There are times when we forget we've left Moscow," two young Russian journalists confessed to us. "You start off at Vova's, then see what's up at Grisha's, then make sure you haven't missed anything at Arkady's. . . . The girls are almost the same too. Oh, every once in a while an American will tag along, but we had our Americans in Moscow."

The largest Russian colony in the metropolitan area is Little Odessa in Brooklyn's Brighton Beach, so called because many of its inhabitants come from in or around the Black Sea port. The artistic crowd, which is largely from Moscow and Leningrad, prefers Manhattan. It tends to revolve around several focal points: the offices of the two main Russian-language newspapers, the Edward Nakhamkin Gallery, the cultural center in SoHo, the Ruslan Café on Madison Avenue, and the Kavkasian Restaurant on Second. When the last establishment innocently opened as the Caucasian Restaurant, it caused quite a stir among the local ethnic populations, which saw it as a proclamation of racial purity. Its name refers, in fact, to the Caucasus Mountains.

New York's ethnic variety, 1980 style, made another strong impression on me. Either it had grown substantially since my first American jaunt five years earlier, or as a Soviet tourist I had simply failed to notice it. Maybe it is easier to notice after you yourself turn into an ethnic minority.

What makes New York an American city is the absence of a common face. Any generalization is bound to miss the mark. Of the scores of accents I found the Filipino most inscrutable. And then there are the unbelievable names— the Jim Gangulas and Rick Zyzzes—whose origins are sometimes lost even to their bearers. An extremely personable gentleman from Madagascar once introduced himself to me as something that sounded more or less like Nameletronkuontrantarisa, but immediately added, "Of course that's impossible. Just call me Mister Désiré." If your name is Whitney, you'll probably be asked to spell it.

"Clearly New York is where the literary refugee is meant to take refuge in this country," I said to Maya. And she agreed. But she also said that she for one did not feel like living in New York. And I agreed.

If we'd stayed in New York, we wouldn't have had to worry about standing out: we could have stayed among our own, our émigré crowd, and what difference does it make what your English sounds like in a town where half the population speaks the language as poorly as you? Émigré life has a bit of the bivouac quality to it, but it's a permanent kind of bivouac, and a feeling of danger goes side by side with the conviction that the danger is not quite mortal. So let's cling to one another on the basis of ethnicity or age or profession or sexual proclivity . . .

"Why have Russian writers singled out New York?" I was asked by Kenneth Woodward of *Newsweek*—one of the few "real" Americans I met during my first several weeks in New York. We were riding up to Columbia University in a taxi. While he concentrated on sharpening his pencil, I gave the matter some thought. Then, just as I was about to reply, our driver stuck his head out of the window and screamed in GPJF (our great-powerful-just-and-free mother tongue, as Turgenev called it), "Yob tvoyu mat, raspizdyai srany! Vzyal moy zelyony!"

Maya and I laughed so hard we nearly fell off our seats. "There's your answer," I panted to my interviewer.

"But what did he say? What did he say?"

The cab driver's New York demotic in my loose translation for the native American ran as follows: "Fuck you, you filthy cunt! Taking my green light!"

When you get down to it, the presence of Russian cab drivers, artists, shopkeepers, musicians, and restaurateurs, the whole multinational stew, the city's unbelievable physical presence, its splendor and misery and crime and punishment, its heartrending love stories and wonder-working lip, its instant deaths, fortuitous encounters, political gambles, and endless quantities and qualities of food and drink—what more could a Russian writer ask for? And since it also houses practically all American book and magazine publishers and in a radius so small, as *The New Yorker* put it a few years ago, that a simple trinitrotoluene bomb could annihilate them all—what writer could fail to be tempted? Still, I felt there was something missing. It was something I couldn't quite put my finger on at the time, but it was important enough to make us decide to push on. And I wasn't the only one. Suddenly it occurred to us that very few Russian émigré writers had ultimately put down roots in New York. "You see?" I said to Maya. "They come and then they go." Many prefer Europe, and the ones who choose America gravitate to university campuses. And even if the America-wide diaspora is due partly to economic factors, the fact remains that our writers make little use of what New York has to offer.

We came up with all kinds of rationalizations for our decision to leave. "If we stay, we'll be stuck in a Russian village. We'll be sucked in. We'll never learn English. And then, who wants to live in the same city as those repulsive megalomaniacs X and Y? And then, look at those prices! Fifteen hundred for a two-bedroom apartment—pretty steep for the privilege of sharing a few small rooms with a large band of cockroaches."

It was quite some time before I realized that, in fact, our decision to leave New York was motivated chiefly by *aesthetic* considerations, or, to be more precise, an aesthetic deficiency either in New York or in ourselves: we had failed to appreciate the phenomenon of America's urban pop.

URBAN POP

I never thought the sight of fire escapes running along a brick wall would plunge me into deep depression, but is there anything sadder than the block after block of rundown walkups stretching across Brooklyn, Manhattan, Queens, Philadelphia, Chicago? A face peering out from one of those narrow casement windows can only be the face of failure. Try to picture a happy couple, a tempting meal, a stimulating book in one of those apartments. Clearly they were built for profit, for Mammon alone, with nary a thought for man's aesthetic needs or, rather, with outright disdain for them. In fact, all the rest of America's urban heritage—the brownstones and town houses with their steep stoops and clumsy columns, the commercial colossi of the late nineteenth century, the early skyscrapers with their pineconed and goat-legged cornices (and their direct influence on the Stalinist style of "architectural excess")—I found purely and simply depressing.

After thinking it all through, I came to the conclusion that what I missed in America was a real city, or rather my own idea of a real city; that is, a European city that had 1) taken shape in history and 2) retained at least a hint of the art nouveau period. Art nouveau—"late Russian modern" in its Russian variant, which originated in Petersburg just before the First World War—is extremely hard to find in America, but it is extremely important for us. As far as I could tell, America was still a mere outpost of civilization at the time, an aesthetic wasteland, an all-purpose factory, a dollar mill.

True, I admired contemporary American architecture and its commitment to the presence of a free body standing in free space; I also felt a certain stirring at the sight of the best of the Great Gatsby-era buildings; but anything from an earlier period left me cold at best, and I looked on bewildered while all kinds of care was lavished on the restoration of a 1910-era Pennsylvania Avenue house in Washington, D.C.: not even upstart merchants in provincial Kazan or Nizhny Novgorod would have paid good money to put up a house with such monstrous turrets! No, this country has no nostalgia for its cities, I said to myself; its attitude is strictly utilitarian. That is why the downtown areas of Chicago, LA, and Detroit are so empty after sundown and even much of New York seems to close down.

Later I realized how wrong I was and why. I had almost

completely overlooked the melancholy side of American life, its provincialism, and the concomitant tendency to let its cities go to pot.

Recently I had occasion to see an excellent animated film called *American Pop.* I was surprised to find so much of what I had deemed antiaesthetic, unworthy of attention—fire escapes, gaps between buildings plugged up with garbage pails, porches with potbellied columns, and row upon row of narrow windows—brought together to make an urban aesthetic whole of its own. I was reminded of an American novel I had once read, a novel in which the protagonist, returning from Europe after the war, catches sight of a pile of Coca-Cola cases on the pier and bursts into a paroxysm of patriotism.

To appreciate American urban pop, you have to grow up with it, and when we refugees, wrenched from our former worlds, make new lives for ourselves, they must bear at least some resemblance to the ones we used to live. Even the most devoted Russian America lovers among us felt alienated from the local pop culture when we experienced it firsthand. Not until we came to America did we learn that, yes, we really were Europeans.

AMERICAN FRUSTRATIONS

Once we went up to Sarah Lawrence College in Bronxville, just outside of New York, for a concert of Russian chamber music. The half-hour ride from Grand Central Station deserves a few lines.

After rumbling through endless tunnels, the train surfaced amid the ruins of Stalingrad, also known as the South Bronx. Picture gaping windows of burned-out—or was it bombed-out—buildings, deserted streets overrun with weeds, an alleycat crossing a dump (I shudder to think of the life it leads), here and there a decrepit hole in the wall with a crooked COLD BEER sign hanging over the door, and a bunch of multiracial down-and-outers hanging out in front—perfect illustrations for the most vehement anti-American propaganda sheet. Picture a Soviet who has never believed a word of that propaganda set down by some miracle in the middle of the South Bronx and told, "Welcome to America!" The first thing he would do is cover his eyes and moan, "So *they* weren't lying. It really is the way *they* say it is."

Don't worry. They *were* lying. Stay on the train a few more minutes and you'll come to Bronxville, the real America of neat little towns, well-stocked gas stations and supermarkets, spacious shopping centers, and white clapboard houses. America's prosperity becomes apparent the moment you leave her large cities. In Russia the opposite is the case. What remains after the military has drained off most of the resources goes toward maintaining a minimal level of decency in the cities; the countryside and villages are left to rot.

The South Bronx is a good example for the Russian émigré of America's notorious "urban crisis" and, in its own paradoxical way, of the failure of Soviet anti-American propaganda. From the standpoint of the Russian refugee, the South Bronx phenomenon simply cannot exist (except, perhaps, as a phantom of Soviet propaganda); in fact, *no* negative features of American life can exist. Soviet propaganda has piled up so many lies in its lifetime that it now gives reverse results: a certain brand of "critically thinking" Soviet citizen—and most of the new émigrés fall into the pattern—no longer believes a word of it; the critically thinking Soviet rejects both the lies of Soviet propaganda and the scraps of truth the propaganda machine needs to make the lies appear true.

If, for example, Soviet newspapers or Soviet television does a report on unemployment in the United States (and reports on unemployment in the United States are all but daily media fare), the critically thinking Soviet (CTS) will typically react with something along the lines of "Wouldn't it be nice to live like their unemployed?" In a sense he is right, of course, but he is wrong too, and it is Soviet propaganda that prevents him from seeing why.

Another example: As soon as the CTS hears a word about American slums, he smiles sarcastically. "I bet they're castles compared with our *khrushchoby.*" (*Khrushchoby* is Soviet slang for the slap-dash apartment buildings that went up during the Khrushchev era; it is a pun on *trushchoby,* the Russian word for slums.) In this instance he is very definitely wrong: Soviet apartments may be cramped, but for the most part they are perfectly satisfactory and equipped with the standard conveniences; they have nothing in common with South Bronx housing projects.

When the Soviet press runs stories about the American crime rate or the American drug scene, the CTS brushes them aside. "The crap *they* dish up to us. Anything to discredit America." And making fun of television coverage of America has become a cliché. "All we see is fires, explosions, and plane accidents. If we're lucky, we get a natural disaster." What they don't realize is that American television shows much the same thing and that there is little or no attempt to put any "positive" news on the screen.

In any case, as a direct result of anti-American propaganda the CTS forms a picture of America as an ideal society, prosperous and romantic. America is the country of "Stardust" and "Serenade in Blue." Thousands of Soviet émigrés were cruelly disappointed with what they found instead.

Many Russian émigrés have trouble grasping what it means to be held up or mugged. Some let out a scream at the sight of a gun and get a panic bullet for their candor; others attack and watch their amazed attackers turn and make tracks. It has taken time for Russians to learn that the most dynamic and prosperous parts of town may border directly on neighborhoods full of crime and decay, that a crowd of courteous, smiling people may hide a maniac with a knife.

Another surprise, even shock, for many émigrés is the American variety of boredom. Boredom was the last thing they feared; it never entered their minds. How can anyone be bored in a city with a frontier name like Indianapolis or a state whose name exudes adventure like Minnesota? And then all those exotic blazing signs along the roads—Pizza Hut, Burger King, Exxon, K mart, Grand Union—and their enormous parking lots waiting to receive you, and the long strings of headlights whizzing past. And suddenly you realize it's all a treadmill, it's the sticks, it's loneliness.

But my greatest surprise was American provinciality. From a distance and through an iron curtain darkly, America of the open borders, America the melting pot, America the global leader seemed like the crossroads of the world, the natural home of cosmopolitanism. We had the feeling that the TV weather report would give the temperature of the water at Nice and the depth of the snow cover on Kilimanjaro, that the news would report on King Carlos's new shoes, the latest intrigues in the central committee of the Chinese Communist party, and the penetration of Marxism into the depths of New Guinea. What we find is that if important international events do make it on the evening news, they are relegated to the end of the program and are glossed over as quickly as possible. The feature of the day is more likely to be a prim young miss telling the world that she was sexually molested twelve years before by the principal of her elementary school, a middle-aged, cauliflower-eared dolt, who categorically denies the accusation.

AMERICAN FASCINATIONS

Of course the fascinations outnumber the frustrations. And how. One of the first things that fascinates Russian émigrés is the food. Not that they are charmed by such American culinary wonders as T-bone steak with apricot preserves, corn on the cob, a chunk of watermelon, and a slice of pineapple smothered with Thousand Island dressing; they simply can't get over the quantity and quality of food available.

When Americans read about food shortages in Russia, they have no clear picture of what is involved. Depending on their political orientation they conjure up either a famine or a late delivery of lobsters. Neither has anything to do with the truth. There is no famine, because there are always *some* comestibles to be had; nor are the lobster deliveries late, because there are no lobsters, and only those Soviet citizens who read foreign novels know of their existence.

Perhaps the following recent story from Moscow, the best supplied city in the Soviet Union, will throw some light on the situation. A man asks an influential friend to get him a kilo of Gruyère. His influential friend sighs and says, "Sorry, but the days of this or that cheese are over. All we have is something called 'cheese,' and I'll do what I can to find you some. If you like, I can try to come up with a bluebird too." A "bluebird" is a chicken.

After such scarcity the groaning supermarket shelves appear miraculous to the Soviet émigré, like the Communist dream come true. For a while the émigré feels slightly dizzy in his local supermarket. Then he starts feeling guilty: think of all the people *there* who are deprived of this abundance.

Some foods are completely new to Soviet émigrés, so new they don't quite know what to do with them. One family from Kiev came to the States with a myth about the miraculous qualities of the "avocado nut." On their first trip to the Safeway they bought some avocados, peeled them, threw away the green slime, and set eagerly upon the "nut" with a hammer.

No sooner do émigrés feel at home in this world of plenty than they start reminiscing about the glories of the Russian cuisine and criticizing Americans for their pale palates.

They begin to patronize Russian shops where they can find "genuine" *tvorog* (a kind of rich, smooth cottage cheese) instead of the American farmer or hoop cheese "imitations," where even the herring is more "genuine." Then they take to counting calories.

Another early—and grandiose—American fascination is the car. To this day owning a car in the Soviet Union is a sign of having made it. At the same time it represents a kind of challenge to the principles of collectivism: car owners are called "privates," *chastniki,* as were the kulaks, the rich peasants who refused to give up their land and join collective farms; automobile theft is commonly referred to as "dekulakification," *raskulachivanie.*

Before coming to the States I had driven a car for ten years—I even wrote a novel about the vagaries of motoring in Russia—and my wife, Maya, as a former member of the Soviet elite, had spent more than twenty years behind the wheel. But we were anything but typical: most of the Soviet émigrés had no experience with cars before leaving their homeland and arrived abroad not knowing how to drive. To them the endlessly flowing river of cars was staggering.

In Los Angeles we heard the story (well, *tall* story) of a Russian who bought himself a jumbo 1971 Ford LTD and learned to work the pedals well enough to get it going and lurch his way onto the Santa Monica Freeway. Afraid to change lanes and unable to read the signs, he drove straight ahead until the tank was empty. In the small California town where he ended up, he 1) found a job, 2) learned English, 3) got married, 4) bought a house, and 5) struck it rich. Now he is a big real estate honcho and tools around in a BMW.

Among the indisputable and unsurpassed fascinations America has to offer is natural beauty. Its variety and state of preservation never cease to amaze us. The hills of Virginia, Kentucky, and Tennessee in their autumn splendor;

the Florida shoreline with its businesslike pelicans and mysteriously mincing herons; the green slopes of Vermont and their affinity to the Caucasus and the Carpathians; the monumental ridges of the Rockies; the stately California sequoias and never-ending California beaches; the mirage-like horizons of Arizona; yes, and the Kansas flatlands—the impression is always one of plenty, of superabundance.

We have driven cross-country twice now, and both times we moved into the heartlands we thought of the pioneers for whom the same journey was tantamount to discovering a new planet. Strange as it may seem, the "new planet" sensation has not yet died out. It is amazing how sparsely populated much of the continent remains, even in the east. Northern Pennsylvania, where for fifty miles at a stretch you will see not a single house, reminded us of parts of Siberia. I would venture to say that America is less densely populated and a good deal less polluted than the Soviet Union, at least than European Russia, the Caucasus, Central Asia, and Southern Siberia. Northern Siberia is of course almost entirely unpopulated, but the Ukraine (I once drove across it from the southeastern to the northwestern tip) has been polluted by chemical plants and heavy industry in a way that exceeds the worst nightmares of Michigan and Massachusetts environmentalists.

Closely related to our fascination with America's landscape is a fascination with her open borders. Although I'm afraid Americans will have trouble appreciating the connection, a Soviet gazing at the horizon cannot help feeling how wonderful it is that the spaces are really open and how unusual that no one is watching and he can go in any or all directions, as far as he pleases. Of course, the fact that Russia's borders are closed, hermetically sealed, lends her landscape an image all its own, but that will not concern us here: the classics of Russian literature fall outside the realm of this book.

.   .   .

When you speak of a society as large as America, you must be on your guard against generalizations. A generalization is like a beautiful but carelessly stitched pillow: the moment you slide it under your head, it starts bulging on one side or the other and soon the stuffing is pouring out like so many contradictions. Even so, it is safe to say that Americans are an outgoing people. In America the smile is still king. When an American stops smiling, his fellow American is likely to ask him what's wrong. The misanthropes among us may say it's all a formality, but whenever I hear that kind of response I think of what my mother once said when someone maligned the French for reducing courtesy to a formality: "Formal courtesy is preferable to heartfelt boorishness."

Now I will venture yet another suspicious generalization; namely, that Americans are more courteous than the French. At least with foreigners. Once in Paris—admittedly, it was in a bad neighborhood—a bartender made such obnoxious fun of my—admittedly—broken French that I exploded back at him in choice Russian. It worked, by the way: he apologized.

Nothing of the sort could happen in America. A foreign accent never triggers annoyance here; people are willing to make the effort to understand. "But that's got nothing to do with their nature," says the skeptic. "It's a fact of their history: they all come from somewhere else—and in the not-so-distant past, either." Be that as it may, the recent émigrés find it an endearing trait.

Once when I was paying for something with a credit card, the salesman asked me whether my name was Polish. "Names that end in '-ov' are Russian," I replied. "Polish names usually end in '-ski.'" Since my salesman and three others nearby seemed interested, I asked them their names. "Gustavo Salazar," my salesman answered. And when I pointed out that he didn't look Spanish (he had an Oriental slant to his eyes), he told me he was Filipino. Two of the other salesmen turned out to be from Iran and Tobago, respectively, and only the third was a native-born American—of Sicilian parentage. We looked at one another and laughed.

Here we live, refugees from everywhere, some fleeing hunger, others bullets, still others the censor. America's ethnic variety knows no equal. We have quickly grown accustomed to it. (When we go to Europe now, we turn up our noses at its ethnic monotony.) If nothing else, the variety helps to remind us that we are not the only ones to have been washed up onto these shores, that we are not alone but part of a community.

It also helps to remind us that America is on the whole freer of xenophobia than any other nation. Americans have their faults (though they sometimes turn into virtues) and their virtues (though they sometimes seem silly to us), but you will never hear an American say, "Damn you foreigners! You're eating us out of house and home!" No, Americans have continued to uphold their tradition of giving shelter and aid to refugees from all parts of the world.

And what a relief for a sweaty, harried refugee to find himself in a society of outgoing, well-wishing, and healthy, physically attractive people. Washing and cleaning are a national perpetuum mobile; jogging and aerobics make American cities look like training camps. America is a nation of good-looking, well-built . . . oops! There goes the generalization pillow again. Because nowhere have I seen so many overweight young people. But more about that elsewhere.

America's fascinating mania for physical fitness has been traced to such diverse sources as pragmatism, hedonism, and narcissism. I would not rule out the possibility of a religious element: for is not the body the means of transport for the soul? Yet I am also fascinated—and delighted—by Americans' willingness to accept and care for disabled bodies: here the religious element is clear. And I have great respect for the way Americans treat their elderly. Their bright clothes—the notorious checked trousers and flower-laden hats—may seem the height of bad taste to jaded Europeans, but they may also reflect a Renaissance-inspired love of life.

In Seattle we once attended a senior citizens' dance where that love of life came out in each foxtrot and jitterbug. It made me think of an incident in a Leningrad dairy shop. When an old woman tried to buy a bottle of milk without waiting her turn, the younger women started shouting, "What are you doing out shopping, you old hag? Why aren't you in the cemetery?" All right, I'll refrain from generalizing, but I can't help drawing parallels.

At first glance it might appear that America does so well by its varied ethnic minority and special interest groups (the handicapped, the aged, and so on) because it believes in equality. I beg to disagree. America believes in "liberty and justice for all," but according to my observations (and I will expand on them later), American society is based on the principle of "benevolent inequality." Yes, I've turned so "reactionary" that I now sing the praises of inequality! If you think about it, though, you'll see that all moves in the direction of socialism here have come to naught: they run contrary to the basic American idea of romantic inequality. True, inequality must be benevolent: it must ensure all members of society the means to maintain their humanity. But once it has done so, inequality is passionate, creative, dynamic.

Equality is static; it squelches all hope for a new and different life. In the Soviet Union you are doomed to the life of a state employee, and unless you turn thief, nothing in your life will change. After all, everyone is equal (except, of course, for those who are more equal). In America, the land of inequality, your chance—the chance for you to change your life—is waiting for you somewhere in the chaos of economic freedom. You may never find it, but the fact that it is there gives your life an entirely different perspective.

Another way of looking at it is to take the etymological approach of a recent émigré. "I used to live on Marx Street in the Lenin district of Stalingrad. I was always in the dumps. Now I live in the State of Maryland, on Rose Garden Street in Silver Spring. I'm sitting on top of the world!"

Sketches for a Novel to Be

1 9 8 0 / "Good morning!"

She doesn't answer. Bernadette Luxe, a smashing two hundred pounds of flesh (plus, as the Russian saying goes, a pound of scorn), spends half the day lolling around in curlers and a lacy peignoir. Given her givens she could easily have produced the ten babies necessary to qualify as the Soviet ideal, a Mother Hero, but she prefers to manage a condominium called the Pacifist Palisades.

I wonder what makes her so standoffish or me so offputting, thinks the HMN. "She never answers when I say good morning to her in the elevator or the lobby. I'll try again . . . No response. Well, forget it." But still, each time he sees her heroic figure either peeking motionless through the peignoir or making Socialist-realist-like waves in the material, he can't help feeling slightly nauseated.

One morning he decides to try something new and combine their two fraternal languages. "Good morning, Zhopa-Novy-God [Ass-New-Year]," he says. Whereupon Bernadette Luxe melts and replies, "Good morning! Nice weather we're having this morning, isn't it? Would you like a pinch of snuff?" The informal approach—it always works. Even when they don't understand what you're saying.

Who is Her Majesty's Navy, and how did he come to America? What do you say? Shall we make him a writer? A Russian writer in exile. Hold on a second. Doesn't that mean we're . . . er . . . writing about ourselves? That's not like us at all. We're not proud. Then let's make him a theater director, okay? Not bad. Takes care of the writer problem. In the Soviet Union he was all the rage; here he's a nobody. Hurray! The Identity Crisis! But he's proud and doesn't force himself on anyone. And since he's gone through more than enough women in his day, he's going it alone. He earns his living as a parking attendant for Colonial Parking, and now that he has saved up a few hundred in tips, he is off to Hawaii.

One more thing: don't think we mean to identify this fifty-year-old with our "melancholy baby." When was the last time you met a baby with a bald spot and a sarcastic smirk?

Of course we might have chosen a younger hero. Fifty-year-olds tend to get on everyone's nerves. Back in the USSR (a phrase we émigrés have taken over from the Beatles) he realized one day in a flash that he was getting on everyone's nerves. Not only he himself but everything connected with him: not only his person, so familiar in "creative circles," but his "daring productions," "original ideas," "impeccable taste," and "high-caliber professionalism." They were sick and tired of him!

But if we do make him younger, it will throw all our chronology off, and that will be the end of the "melancholy baby" motif and the tinkling piano. No, he'll just have to stay fifty and bear the ignominy of starting over as a middle-aged parking attendant at the El Greco. To add insult to injury, the restaurant made a thing of having opened its doors in 1955, the very year the HMN was being trained by the Soviet Navy to land on the American coast a few scant miles away.

1955/ Kronstadt. Navy Bayonet Practice.

Now hear this, lads! All hands on deck!
It's time for weapons practice.
Today you'll learn to plunge bay'nets
Into those NATO-pacters.

America, our enemy,
Is rich, as rich as Croesus,
But due to cap't'list deviltry
The workman's pay decreases.

Don't lunge too high: Yanks love to brawl,
And their strong chests won't spatter;
Go for the juice, go for the balls,
And watch their forces scatter.

The for'ners spurn our Marxist creed,
The science of all sciences;
We *fight for peace: we—pow!—defeat*
All CIA alliances.

So thrust the bayonet in hard:
No more relief we offer
Except abuse by hand or word,
You m-dash, f-dash buggers!

3 From New York we headed west. First stop, Michigan; final destination, Los Angeles, city of surf and writers-in-residence. Michigan and California were known quantities to us; I had been there before and we had friends there. We wondered what it had been like for the thousands of Russians setting off in the seventies, transfixed, after lives lived entirely within the confines of Minsk and Pinsk, by exotic names like Cleveland, Ohio, or Peoria, Illinois. We soon learned that New Minsk and New Pinsk, wherever they happened to be, had been scenes of much weeping and wailing.

We flew to Ann Arbor to spend some time with Carl and Ellendea Proffer, the prime movers of the prime Russian-language publishing venture of the emigration, Ardis Publishers. Our Ardis business done, we performed our first act of American patriotism: we purchased a set of wheels. The choice was between a Volvo and an Omega. The former was the dream of all Moscow crooks; we had no information on the latter except that it had been made by the Oldsmobile branch of the General Motors family in 1980 (a black year for the American automotive industry) and along European lines (which basically meant it did not look like an outsize crocodile).

"It's our duty to buy American," I said to Maya.

"Do you really think one Omega will change anything?"

"It could be the one that tilts the system back in the right direction."

Which is what happened, incidentally. We went to the

local Oldsmobile dealership, wrote the astonished salesman a check for the full amount (we had no inkling of
financing in those days), and drove off. I am convinced to
this day that our Omega (a four-door, six-cylinder automatic) was the one that saved the American automotive
industry, and no one will ever convince me to the contrary.

The Michigan winter differs little from the Russian variety. I'm surprised Michigan hasn't built communism yet.
Since we hadn't emigrated to wallow in snow, we made
tracks south through Illinois, Missouri, Kansas, Oklahoma,
and Texas and then west along the southernmost route,
through New Mexico and Arizona, avoiding the snow in the
Rockies.

It was January, and as we drove, we thought of our pred-
ecessors by almost half a century, the Soviet satirists Ilf and
Petrov, driving across the country in their little gray Ford.
Even then they found amenities the Soviet Union still lacks:
thousands of miles of paved roads; gas stations with cold-
drink vending machines and attendants who wipe your
windshields; roadside cafés; abundant accommodations for
the night. . . . And now I can offer the Soviet reader (if this
book ever has one) an addition to the list of wonders described by Ilf and Petrov in their travelogue. I first came
across it in a cubicle in a remote rest area: a disposable
toilet-seat cover to protect the endangered ass! The sensation it would make in the Soviet Union, where public facili-
ties offer neither toilet paper nor toilet seat! My own
immediate association was the highway police rest stop (on
the two-lane road to the Crimea), where truck drivers squat
to their hearts' content around a shit house boarded up
during the last five-year plan.

The snows stopped in southern Illinois, and we saw no
more of them that winter. I must say we harbored no excess
of sentimental feelings for that form of precipitation anyway. Snow in its aesthetically pure white state—the snow
you find in the countryside—exists for only a few days in

Moscow; for the remaining six months it is as dirty, annoying, and burdensome as the regime itself.

Driving, driving, driving . . . steady movement ahead, on both sides, behind. We took turns at the wheel. Maya complained, "This driving makes me sleepy."

Very quickly we became motel connoisseurs. We did not come across Nabokov's Refuge for Enchanted Hunters, but we did evaluate a slew of Howard Johnsons, Great Westerns, Holiday Inns, and Ramada Inns. We even argued over their good points. Maya preferred HoJos—the breakfasts are better and the TV has more channels. I favored the Holiday Inns for style. But they all had their flaws. On the outskirts of St. Louis I had a chance to prove my point. We had stopped at a "luxurious" HoJo. Our room opened on a gigantic enclosed patio with burbling fountains and crashing waterfalls. A beau could take his belle from the enormous pool to the gigantic video arcade and never wet his feet. The smell of chlorine fumes and incessant electronic beeps kept us up for hours. Maya silently accepted defeat.

We crossed the Texas border at night, stopped at a Howard Johnson, and went down to breakfast the next morning not suspecting where we were. Trained as we are to avoid clichés like the plague, we forget they often have a basis in reality. That morning we were surrounded by faces from the westerns that had made my youth: there sat John Wayne, Gregory Peck, Gene Autry. I had seen them too many times to be mistaken. And although I can only suppose that most if not all of them were truck drivers, they dressed in the same hats, vests, and boots as their cowboy antecedents.

The waitress brought us juice, eggs (which turned out to be a "side" of eggs), two stacks of bacon, toast, griddle cakes, butter, syrup, and jam. "I was wondering, folks," she drawled as she unloaded her tray, "what language that is you're talking."

"What do you think?" I asked.

"Sounds mighty like German."

"No. Russian."

"Just what I thought," she said. "Russian or German."

"They're actually quite different; they don't sound at all alike."

"Really?" She was sincerely surprised. "You mean you're Russians from Germany."

"No, we're from Russia."

"Germans from Russia?"

In the mind of this middle-aged Texas woman, Russians and Germans were inextricably intertwined. We outlined the historical clashes between the two nations, arguing for the supremacy of Byzantine culture over Gothic (or vice versa) and stressing that whereas the Germans had invented a spout for the Russian samovar, there was still a popular Russian saying to the effect that "what's good for a Russian is bad for a German."

Shaking her head in confusion, she went over to a group of "cowboys" and, pretending to clear their table, told them about the weirdos at table four: they say they come from Russia, but they're not German. The men turned to have a look at us, but the moment our eyes met they averted theirs, pretending to study the weather outside.

When the waitress came up to us again, she looked worried. "The fellows, they say the papers print a lot about Russia. A lot of nasty stuff. Are the papers lying?"

"Afraid not."

"The fellows say that Russia has the type of government that doesn't permit you to write the books you want. Is that so?"

I was astounded. What a question to be asked in Sweetwater, Texas!

"Yes, ma'am, that unfortunately is also true. You see, I'm a writer and the government kicked me out for writing books it didn't like. That's why we're here."

Suddenly the waitress threw open her arms and said with

a warmth I count among the greatest of American charms, "Welcome to America!"

The cowboys smiled reservedly.

THE DAY I LOST MY CITIZENSHIP

The last day of our journey turned into an important landmark in my biography: on January 21, 1981, just after sunset, I learned I was no longer a citizen of the USSR.

I awoke that morning a Soviet citizen like any other, except that I awoke in Yuma, where Arizona, California, and Mexico come together. With the dignity prescribed by the Directorate of Visas of the Moscow Municipal Council I bore the lofty title of representative of the Land of the Soviets into the dining room. Once on the road, however, just past the point where the Arizona desert segues into the California desert, I disgraced my country by committing a terrible crime: I sped past the bristling mustache of a highway patrolman. The next thing I knew, the red lights on the roof of his car were flashing like mad in my rearview mirror.

I had no choice but to pull the Omega over to the shoulder.

We got out of the cars, I and this slender cowboy armed with handcuffs, walkie-talkie, and a six-shooter. Two desert eagles soared above us in the empty skies.

Here comes trouble, I thought as he approached. I haven't got a single American document. A Soviet citizen and so close to the Mexican border. If an American was caught in Turkmenia along the Iranian border, the whole KGB would be out in no time. What will he think when he sees a Soviet passport, a different alphabet? Should I tell him the story behind *The Burn* and how I tried to publish an independent literary miscellany, or should I play dumb, as I did back home in comparable situations?

"License and registration, please."

"You see, officer, we're from Russia, the Soviet Union,

I mean . . ." Grimly I handed him the little booklet that was my driver's license (Soviet licenses are as different from American ones as *Pravda* is from the *New York Times*). "It's a Soviet license, and . . ."

"How do you spell your name?" he asked, calmly examining the license and noting the number.

Once I'd wound my tongue around the spelling, the patrolman looked up from his notes and said, "So you're from Russia, sir?"

Yes, I was, but we were here by virtue of extraordinary circumstances, which I'd be only too glad to . . .

"Do you know what the speed limit is here?" he interrupted me again.

"Fifty-five miles an hour."

"Correct."

"You see, the USSR has no speed limits," I lied, "and . . ."

"You're not in Russia now, are you, sir? You're in America. And we do have a speed limit, okay?"

A Kiev policeman had once grumbled at me in the same way. "This isn't Moscow; this is Kiev, see? *Our* laws apply here, got it?"

That reminded me of a psychological trick my Moscow friends had taught me: try to make his beat something important, something special. "I've never driven the desert before! What a thrill! Before you know it, you're up to sixty-five and . . ."

"Seventy-five."

"Are you going to fine me?" I asked, defeated at last.

"I don't fine you; the court does." He handed me a ticket. "But I've put you down for only sixty-five. Be more careful in the future. So long and drive safely!"

The moment he turned away he lost all interest in me. Only then did I realize that I wasn't a suspicious foreigner to him at all; I was a man like any other. I had simply broken the speeding law.

As I drove away, still troubled by this dispute over rights,

I had a premonition that I would soon be involved in a second nasty episode and that it too would involve a violation of rights—only this time mine.

By evening we had reached the house of an old friend in Santa Monica. We were greeted with the news that reporters had been after me all day. "I'm sorry to have to tell you this, Vasya, but the Presidium of the Supreme Soviet of the USSR has stripped you of your citizenship."

Well, well, I thought as I walked along the beach to calm myself. So the ideological apparatchiks reclining in their saunas have decreed me out of house and homeland, deprived me of my forty-eight years in Russia, a Kazan orphan with living parents in the camps, a Magadan adolescent, a Leningrad medical student, a Moscow writer. Funny, I hadn't even broken the law, yet to them I was *not* a man like any other.

I could see the twinkling lights of the Pacific Coast Highway. Why did the statesmen of the USSR do this to me? Had my works upset them so much? Had I encroached on their authority? They could gorge themselves on their power if they wanted to.

Back at my host's I found a houseful of people, most of them friends from UCLA, where I had given a seminar in 1975. In the six years that had passed they had not changed at all, but that was no trick: in California, teachers are as well preserved as movie stars.

At the height of the festivities I had a call from New York. It was Craig Whitney, a former Moscow correspondent, then head of the foreign desk at the *New York Times*. He wanted to know how I felt about losing my citizenship and whether I had anything to say to the Soviet authorities. I shouted my message over the din. Craig laughed. The morning edition of the *Times* carried it as follows, "Having been informed about the government's decision, Aksyonov said, 'To hell with them!'"

CALIFORNIA RESERVATIONS

California, Los Angeles, Hollywood, Sunset Strip. It doesn't take a Pegasus of an imagination to kick up its heels and take flight. Then comes the wet blanket, the neutron bomb effect: streets that expire after dark, houses that tremble behind ARMED RESPONSE signs. It's another of America's vicious circles: people stay home at night because they fear attackers; empty streets attract attackers. "Get out of the house!" we felt like shouting. "Get into the streets and watch the muggers melt, the burglars bolt! Put some life back into the city! Don't hide away in restaurants! Open outdoor cafés! The climate is made for it!"

But perhaps LA is merely a radically different mode of urban existence, one the rest of us are not yet quite attuned to. Nowhere is American urban pop so strongly entrenched. Instead of the prevailing catch-as-catch-can jumble, picture magnificent terraces leading down to the ocean, picture luxury hotels lining the shore front. Now picture the ugly, dumpy, utilitarian structures extending for miles on end along commercial boulevards like Pico, Lincoln, Ventura, streets where billboards take the place of architecture. We couldn't help feeling that Los Angeles was a town designed by people oblivious to town planning and history.

Nor could we picture ourselves living forever in a town that for all its creative potential gave the impression of being totally cut off from culture, from life in general. In 1975, when I was in California for the first time, I was, as the natives say, "blown away" by the mythology of the place, so much so that I failed to grasp the reality behind it; this time I kept thinking we had plunged into an ankle-deep existence. We thought perhaps the film world would change our minds: movie people were always live wires. But all the Hollywood parties we attended were lugubrious, businesslike affairs. Even Eros was out to lunch. Everyone's eyes seemed glazed over with dollar signs.

No, we couldn't quite picture ourselves living forever in a town where Jaguars and Rolls-Royces were as everyday an occurrence as motorcycles in Moscow or mink coats in New York, which in turn are as popular as musquash-imitation rabbit hats in Novosibirsk, which are about as ordinary as, say, bicycles in Beijing, where the bicycle population is, naturally, on a par with the population of Jaguars and Rolls-Royces in Los Angeles—and thanks for sticking with me through so convoluted a sentence.

In any case, a few months in LA and we were back on the road. I had completed a semester stint as writer-in-residence at the University of Southern California, and the Kennan Institute for Advanced Russian Studies, a branch of the Wilson Center at the Smithsonian Institution in Washington, had offered me a year's fellowship. So we pulled up stakes and moved on. On and on across California, Arizona, Utah, Colorado, Kansas, Missouri, Illinois, Ohio, West Virginia, and Maryland—and on into the no-star, nonstate of the District of Columbia. Little did we realize that our gypsy days were over.

Sketches for a Novel to Be

1 9 8 0 / Bernadette's boyfriend, insurance agent Randolph Golenzo, hearing about the new tenant, musters everything he's heard about Russia, which—and this he knew for a fact—is also called Soviet Georgia. "Russia is a country of enormous strength situated between China and Germany. Not all Russians are Georgians, honeybun. Nikita Khrushchev was a Georgian. Georgians are the elite, like our Wasps. But they sting harder! Ha ha ha! They've been discussing the question of the Georgification of Africa in their party synagogues for the last century. Some people are incensed by the occupation of Afghanistan, but I have a feeling that the conflict's been resolved once and for all by a recent conference in Atlanta."

The plumber and air-conditioning supervisor at the Pacifist Palisades is a refugee Vietnamese general by the name of Pxi, who weighs in at just under a hundred pounds. A garland of keys and wrenches jingles from his belt, which he wears cowboy style, low on the hip. Bernadette Luxe admires the general. "Tiny Pxi retreated with gun in hand," she tells her Randy. He is obviously jealous. "When you've got a gun in your hand, honeybun, you don't retreat; you attack."

The general can often be seen in the vestibule near the globe, spinning our planet in minature with a miniature finger, his attention focused on the Arctic basin, which is understandable in part.

Entrenched though he is in the Pacifist Palisades, the HMN still manages to come in contact with the life of the real America. In fact, every day he picks up some new tidbit. Here are a few examples.

One morning his neighbor, a Robert Redford look-alike, says to his wife, a Victoria Principal look-alike, "You're terrific, dear, but your breath is unbearable. Here, have a Clorets. Now your mouth smells like a bunch of exotic flowers. Remember that time in Bermuda? Quick, draw the blinds!"

In the parking lot, after a busy day, the Linda Evans look-alike neighbor runs into the Joan Collins look-alike neighbor. "You look tired, dear," she says. "Yes, I've had a rough day. First, my boss, then two salesmen from Ohio. My tennis partner at lunch, and the French pastry chef after work." "The only reason you're tired, dear, is that you don't use Freshotton tampons. Look at me—I'm fresh as a daisy after seven appointments."

Twilight. The penthouse resident, a Bert Lancaster look-alike, sits with his long drink on the balcony. Tenderly, caressingly, he gazes into the bedroom where his wife, a Shirley MacLaine look-alike, is nourishing her smashing face with the sweet-smelling Oil of Olay. Time listens to Oil of Olay, he thinks. A pity I can't use it myself.

A couple of confirmed bachelors meet in the morning, as energetic as young boys. "Everything okay, Doug?" asks the Bert Reynolds look-alike. "Just fine, Steve! It used to itch something fierce, but after I took your advice and tried that wonderful Preparation-H, it vanished into thin air. Now I'm ready to start a new day!"

A Lee Iacocca look-alike car dealer is overcome by

a strange mood every Friday. "I'll sell everything cheap when I'm in this mood," he shouts. "You and your moods!" his wife shouts back. "You'll ruin us!" "Impossible!" he screams. "Come and buy my cars while I'm in the mood!"

4 My wife, Maya, was born in Moscow and I chalked up twenty-five years there before being booted out. We knew what life in a world capital was like. Our Angeleno friends warned us to be prepared for something less in Washington: "In many respects it's just a Southern backwater. You say they want you for a year? Well, you have our sympathy." We were worried: if Los Angeles seemed a backwater to us, what would we make of Washington?

Yet we took to the place from the first. Perhaps it satisfied one minor complex from the émigré's bouquet of same. Here on Capitol Hill, between the Congress and its library, with colonnades competing against trees on every side, you can recall stately St. Petersburg; walking along the brightly painted façades of Georgetown, you can approximate a Britain that still exists; sitting in a sidewalk café in Dupont Circle, you can catch the universal Parisian spirit. Was it the call of the capital? An imperial imperative?

Although many of my Moscow friends felt entirely at home in SoHo's muddy waters, I now confirmed what I had always suspected: that I was no birthright bohemian. I found a strange harmony in Washington's official surroundings, and suddenly everything fell into place. "Feeling homesick for the old empire?" a New York friend inquired. But that wasn't it at all. What I liked, for example, was the Gothic of St. Dominic's in the perspective of well-balanced contemporary lines. The "old empire" would sooner have gone under than put up abstract sculptures in and among its ministries and miscellaneous sanctuaries. After all, an abstract sculpture might just lead the observer to a few abstract thoughts (thoughts of his own) and thence to a rejection of the pretenses the empire lives by.

We immediately crossed the prestigious Georgetown off our list of residential possibilities (its Victorian town houses meant nothing to us at the time) and decided instead on a high rise in the southwestern part of town. "That makes sense," our new Washington friends told us. "You'll be close to the Wilson Center." With time, though, we realized we had chosen the neighborhood not so much because it was close to the Wilson Center as because it was close—in a different sense of the word—to certain soulless sections of Moscow. How ironic that we should feel nostalgia for a purely functional living space. We even started calling it "Startown," the people's name for the area just outside Moscow—an enclave of clean, uncluttered, well-landscaped streets—where the cosmonauts live.

Another point of similarity: the Washington circles we moved in did not differ greatly from a segment of our Moscow acquaintances—the diplomats, journalists, Slavists, political scientists, in sum, the people we thought of at home as "our Americans" or "our foreigners." That they were no longer foreigners was hard for us to grasp. In fact, Russian émigrés, no matter where they are, tend to think of the local population as "foreign." But then, all members of large nations find it impossible to conceive of themselves as aliens.

From time to time I have the strangest encounters at Washington parties. A high-ranking diplomat will suddenly come up to me like an old pal and say, "Good to see you, Vasya! Remember 1966?"

"Now let me see. Wasn't that the one that came just after 1965 and ended with 1967?"

"You mean you don't remember the time a whole bunch of us went to the Novodevichy Monastery Easter service with a suspicious-looking bearded longhair in tow. The KGBeatnik we called him."

"Why, of course! It's been ages"—as the incident falls into place with the old pal's name—"Bill."

There were times when I felt the continual round of parties during those first few months in Washington merging into one unwieldy "multiparty system." Washingtonians outdo even Californians in hospitality. They are hot on the tails of the world champs—the Georgians (the Caucasus Georgians whose capital is Tiflis; I haven't had much experience with Atlantans yet), who long ago won my heart with the toast "And now let's drink the health of our guest, the famous writer What-Was-Your-Name-Again-My-Friend!"

Washingtonians apparently need to keep reminding one another they live in the nation's capital, but given the current rate—and quality—of development they may soon put their inferiority complex behind them. Some have already begun. A Washington guest at a large New York party I recently attended maintained that New York was provincial in comparison with Washington (the proximity of New York is a particular sore spot for Washingtonians). Of course the New Yorkers were immediately on his back: "New York is the crossroads of the world. It's literature and theater, it's fashion, it's everything!" But the Washingtonian just smiled as if to say, "It won't be long before they see what I mean."

City rivalry is nothing new to Russians. Moscow and Petersburg were at loggerheads for ages. In 1905 a group of Moscow millionaires stirred up a rebellion (now known as the First Russian Revolution) against the Petersburg aristocrats. The revolt was put down by the Guards Regiments, but the Moscow-Petersburg rivalry went on unabated. The Bolsheviks preferred Moscow because it was farther from the border. Besides, its Byzantine pomp and splendor tallied well with communism's penchant for loud and tasteless self-glorification. Yet there are scholars who maintain that a return to Petersburg is only a matter of time.

In America, fortunately, nothing so drastic is at stake. The rivalry has more to do with which city is more cosmopolitan. And it must be said that there are places in Washington where without a bit of prompting no one would ever believe he was in the capital of the United States, that is, of the free world, that is, of contemporary humanity. The hovels, the bumpy roads, the withering trees . . . a dusty, rusty image from the Godforsaken South. But all that is now being pushed farther and farther from the heart of the city, giving way to an architecture and rhythm worthy of a great capital. You can even feel it in the way people walk.

And the changes are taking place before our very eyes. We have seen mirror-fronted buildings going up and slums coming down; we have seen the formerly seedy shore-front section of Georgetown turn into a stylish, vaguely bohemian playground à la Greenwich Village (only better) or the Latin Quarter (not nearly so good as yet); we have seen Dupont Circle burgeon with sidewalk cafés. After visiting a number of American cities, I can say without compunction that Washington has one of the liveliest street scenes— day or night.

Not long ago I happened to be at the Georgetown intersection of M and 19th with the poet William Jay Smith, who had lived in Washington a few years before while serving as poet-in-residence at the Library of Congress. "I don't recognize the place," he told me. "You used to see nothing but cats at night, cats and an occasional shadow that ran for shelter at the sight of another. And now look at it! Why, it's another St. Germain-des-Prés!" As we looked around, we saw streams of pedestrians as well as streams of cars, we saw every sidewalk café table occupied, we saw a long line of young people waiting to get into Rumors, a singles bar where even the flies used to die of boredom but which is now so popular that the management has opened a branch a few blocks (and a few score restaurants) away, offering free shuttle service between the two.

Actually, it takes only one building—say, the east wing of the National Gallery with its acute angles—to start the cosmopolitan juices flowing. And if Washington still lacks a Champs-Élysées, it will soon have a brand-new Pennsylvania Avenue with fancy sidewalks, fountains, glass, restored architectural monuments like the old post office and the Hotel Willard, and plenty of room for parades up to the Capitol. Whether it can sustain an Elysian atmosphere, however, remains to be seen.

In fact, the only thing left of the city's former provinciality is its execrable climate, the sticky, backwoods humidity of its air. Why the clammiest corner of the continent had to be chosen as the nation's capital is not clear to me, but perhaps the new cosmopolitan breeze will have an effect on atmospheric as well as social conditions.

Nowhere is Washington free of politics. Even your fellow joggers turn out to be congressmen or at least political commentators. (Public figures are not to be seen running through the streets of Moscow with their trousers off; they prefer riding fully and conservatively dressed behind the cream-colored blinds of their limousines.) Politics is present even in the preconcert crowd at the Kennedy Center. There goes the assistant assistant of the third subsecretary drifting slowly and elegantly toward the chief deputy of the junior supervisor. Don't be surprised to overhear a strategic discussion of economic sanctions against the Jaruzelski regime as you decide whether to order mushu pork in a Chinese restaurant, and the conversation at a Georgetown party may easily slip into comparative tanks and the cost of an American model (in rubles) and its Soviet counterpart (in dollars). If you happen to be Russian, you are sure to be called in as an instant expert, and you will have no choice but to advise the interested parties either to use the black market rate (that is, four rubles to the dollar) or, even better, to calculate the number of pairs of Levi's to the tank.

And if you'd like a sightseeing tour, well, here's the building where the space shuttle plans are made, there's the building where your dollars are printed, there's the building where those dollars are counted. And yes, that's right, the road sign we saw just now does say PENTAGON. There's a CIA sign too. In the Soviet Union those words are meant to frighten little children; here they are nothing but freeway exits.

THE FLAG TOWER

The building of the Smithsonian Institution in the middle of the mall looked vaguely familiar to me. It is the kind of building that picture postcards and travel brochures imprint on your mind though you can never quite pinpoint it. My first reaction was to ruminate yet again on the vagaries of fate: if anyone had told me a few years ago I would soon be invited to work here and given an office in the main tower, I would have thought the idea as preposterous as an invitation to work in Stalin's old Spassky Tower Kremlin office.

The Wilson Center attracts scholars from all over the world. It brings them to Washington and provides them with a study, a typewriter, a research assistant, and enough of a stipend to lead a modest existence while they work. And work they do, on an amazingly broad range of topics— for instance, "The Influence of Price Stability in the Brazilian Rice Market on the Fluctuation in Australian Tobacco Prices" or "A Comparative Study of the Behavior and Dress of Russian Youth in the 1860s and American Youth in the 1960s." When I proposed to shake up the rational, scholarly atmosphere and write a *novel* in the tower, I was pleasantly surprised to learn that the indulgence of the American academic community knows no bounds.

The tower, a narrow affair topped by a clock and flag, housed three offices, one above the other. Mine was in the middle; below me there was a Frenchman, above me a Chinese. I had no idea what they were working on, but I suspected it was something towering, something about the building of socialism in France or of capitalism in the People's Republic of China. We rode up and down in an old-fashioned elevator with a manual gate and door. Even though Liz Dixon, whose post was at the base of the tower, assured us that it was the safest elevator in town, I couldn't help wondering what would happen if there was a nuclear attack. And clearly I wasn't the only one: just in case, the floor of each office (and therefore the ceiling of the lower two) sported a trap door. In other words, my Chinese colleague would land on my head and the two of us would land on our French colleague.

Seriously, though, the year I spent at the Kennan Institute was enjoyable and fruitful. What a blessing to be in a place where you don't get under anyone's skin and no one interferes with you; how pleasant to spend a year in the company of affable, intelligent people, people who are interested in what you are up to but never nosy, and who are accustomed to a cosmopolitan atmosphere and to names that sound peculiar to the locals.

Actually, I had been friends with James Billington, the director of the center, for more than fifteen years. On a thirty-degree-below-zero (Celsius) day in 1965, I had a visit in Moscow from a red-cheeked professor in a flimsy black coat, Oxford scarf, and bright ("all-weather," as he called it, though it seemed right for any weather but the one at hand) cap. Because the frost seemed determined to keep us company through the city, I gave Jim one of my numerous fur hats; he gave me his cap in exchange. Just before he left, he showed me a large suitcase and told me it contained the manuscript of his magnum opus, *The Icon and the Ax*, a cultural history of Russia. As evidence he pulled out a sheaf of papers, at which point a puff of icy wind came along and blew the papers up over the monument to the founder of scientific communism, K. Marx. While Jim and I ran all over trying to save his labors from the jaws of the Russian winter, his wife, Marjorie, and their three young children looked on at what must have seemed to be a symbolic scene.

A word about the fate of the headgear I always thought of as the "James Billington All-Weather Cap." Very early in the Prague spring—the first drops had only just begun to fall from the roofs—I gave it to a top-notch pianist in the bar of the Jalta Hotel in Prague. He in turn gave it to a Scandinavian saxophone player, who passed it on to someone else, and on it went until finally it came back to me in Moscow with a note from a Japanese judo champion. The last I saw of it, it was sailing over the Baltic Sea: a hurricane wind had knocked it off my head on the island of Saaremaa.

Neither Jim nor Marjorie had changed in the intervening years, though their children had aged considerably: they were now physically and mentally mature college students.

The Kennan Institute of the Wilson Center is devoted to advanced studies of Russia and Eastern Europe. It comprises three rooms and a library with a round table. The library is well stocked with émigré and Soviet editions, and as the Parisian writer Viktor Nekrasov says, reading *Pravda* is the most effective medicine for nostalgia. Perhaps even more effective, though, are the official visits of Soviet scholars and diplomats with their highly guarded behavior. One of them, a fairly good friend in the past, sat a few feet away from me during a seminar one day and looked through me with such skill that I began feeling positively incorporeal.

The head of the institute for that year, Abbott Gleason, seemed to be constantly on the move with "development work," an American euphemism—I explain to my Russian friends—that means "to go begging." Although I now see what an everyday occurrence it is here, I found it quite surprising at first. Passing the hat is a matter of great shame in the Soviet Union. Of course, there's nobody to pass it to but the state. The labyrinthine system of private grants and subsidies is completely new to a Soviet émigré, and I must say I have been amazed at how fast some of my fellow ex-Soviets take to it.

During my stay at the Wilson Center the world of socialism was represented by two individuals, both of whom were
surrounded by a certain mist of ambiguity. One of them, a
professor at Warsaw University, was forced by the Decem-
ber 1981 military coup to wonder whether he was still a
visiting scholar or had turned political refugee. The other,
my flag tower neighbor, held a high post in the Ministry of
Foreign Affairs of the People's Republic of China, and what
is going on there—and was going on there at the time—I
haven't the faintest idea. The "blue ants" of yesteryear are
suddenly becoming Westernized at the speed of the great
leap forward. I first saw my neighbor at a sherry hour sipping Bristol Cream in a Brooks Brothers suit with Confu-
cian inscrutability. When Professor Gleason introduced me
to him, he mentioned that I had been deprived of my Soviet
citizenship for my writings. I had a feeling the whole thing
was an experiment to see how the man would react. What
happened was that his formerly blank face showed signs of
sympathy, which he then expressed in words along with
puzzlement at the motives behind so absurd an act. In other
words, high party member that he was, he was first and
foremost a diplomat, and his reaction was worthy of a member of the House of Lords or, at least, the Russian State
Duma.

The sherry hour ritual in the institute's rotunda is an
integral part of the Wilson process. Every day at noon the
fellows congregate in more or less circular fashion (as more
or less befits the room's configuration) around a circular
table covered with bottles of sherry and stacks of circular
plastic sherry glasses.

When a Russian émigré scholar who turned up at one of
these gatherings asked me, the old-timer, what in the world
was going on, I patiently filled him in on the British tradition of sherry tippling. "So it's sherry, is it?" He sighed,
enshrouded in a gloom quite philosophical. Not so long
before, he had attended regular and compulsory party

meetings at his institute in the Soviet Academy of Sciences, meetings not known for their sherry; now a convinced anti-Communist, he was concerned about the West's ability to stand up to the Soviet Union. "Making small talk and guzzling sherry, having a grand old time, while totalitarianism advances from all sides!"

"Calm down," I told him. "It's just a tradition. Nothing serious. No May Day parade. When the hour is up, they'll all go back to their offices and to shining their grandfathers' rifles. Totalitarianism shall not pass!"

Émigré intellectuals maintain a critical, even supercilious, attitude toward American academic life, especially if they had dreamed of it from afar as an ideal. They are most critical when it comes to the American approach to the study of communism and Soviet politics, to Kremlinology in general. "They don't understand a thing," say some. "They're impossibly naïve," say others. And they all wonder why these Americans lack the sense to lap up their wise counsel.

During the year I spent at the Kennan Institute, however, I was in constant contact with American experts on things Russian and Soviet and I am of a completely different opinion. I was especially impressed by American departments of Slavic languages and literatures. American Slavists are the finest in the world; they even surpass their Soviet counterparts. Of course, there is much variety in the depth of both research and teaching; not all links in the complex chain of university departments and language schools can be uniformly strong. A few members of the field treat it as if it were mineralogy, and one such "expert" is known to have admitted in his cups that he preferred to teach Russian like Greek or Latin—as a dead language. By and large, however, the breadth of output and offerings is unmatched.

I recently attended a conference of the American Association for the Advancement of Slavic Studies, an organization that brings together not only Slavists but also experts in all branches of the Soviet and East European field. The Capitol Hilton, where the conference was held, was so filled with excitement and commitment that it put me in mind of the national Republican and Democratic conventions.

When émigrés (or others) argue that American Sovietology is not yet on a par with Soviet Americanology, I always beg to differ. Every Wednesday for a year I attended talks on Soviet affairs at the Wilson Center, and I can state categorically that Moscow's USA and Canada Institute would drool over the range—and, of course, objectivity—of the material I heard there. Self-confident as the institute may be, its staff is stymied by ideological restrictions, travel restrictions (some of its top-ranking scholars have never been considered reliable enough to earn a visit to the country they spend their life studying), and, most of all, the necessity of feeding the central committee information that supports its preconceived view of the world.

The main restriction faced by American Sovietologists is the Soviets' all but idiotic compulsion for secrecy. In the Soviet press the letter "N" (in the Latin alphabet) stands for something that for strategic reasons may not be mentioned by name. "Here we are in Yalta," the satirists Ilf and Petrov once wrote, "on the shore of the N Sea." American scholars have broken the "N" barrier and even made Soviet secrecy a topic for research. But in the end perhaps all we can say is that while neither side knows much about the other, the Americans are at least more active than the Soviets.

And so I spent a year in that semimysterious, red-brick, stained-glass, many-turreted, ivy-covered building. By the time the year came to an end, the Chinese diplomat had finished his work and gone back to Beijing, the French scholar had finished his work and gone back to Paris, and I, having finished my *Paperscape*, made ready to leave the tower—and settle in Washington for good. Just before I moved out, the secretary of the center, Fran Hunt, told me about another resident of the tower, a permanent one. His "office" was higher than the other three; in fact, it was all the way up in the attic. Legend has it that he was an old owl that had flown up from the South shortly after the building was completed, about 150 years ago, and from that time forth had ventured out only by night. And by night, whenever the flag flapped in the southern breeze, the hoary fellow could still be seen making his way through the embrasure and plunging into a stream of air. I like to think of him as the most "advanced" thinker in the whole Wilson Center and perhaps in the whole District of Columbia.

THE MULTIPARTY SYSTEM

Friday night is party night. Our destination is Georgetown's O Street, where a Mr. and Mrs. Benjamin Reginald Cooper-Clark(!) have requested the honor of our presence.

Maya usually bites her tongue through the Friday evening parking process. Keeping absolutely quiet is the only way she can keep from breaking out into abuse. When the going gets really rough, however, she'll come out with something like, "Couldn't we have called a cab this once?" At which point I inevitably find a spot and squeeze in.

The brick sidewalks of century-old tree-lined O Street click with high heels and swish with fashionably baggy trousers. We can make out at least three brightly lit doorways with guests being shown in. Parties, parties everywhere!

We find ours. "Welcome! Welcome!" cry our hosts. "How are you? Looking great, both of you!" The husband immediately takes me off to the side and says, "Well?" and raising his eyebrows and pointing his head in a southeasterly direction, that is, in the general direction of the government office buildings, he adds, "How do you like it?" "Fantastic," I say. "My sentiments exactly," he agrees. As the conversation progresses, I notice he is looking past my right ear. "Now let me introduce you to our main attraction," he says at last, but just then a new couple arrives and he runs off apologizing.

"Are you sure we're at the right party?" Maya asks me when we are together again.

"Of course I'm sure. Look, there's Greg and Heidi, there's Mel with his mouth full, and isn't that the Princess Trubetskaya sipping beer? It's our crowd, all right, but with a lot of new faces."

The new faces, about sixty in all, are crammed into the living room and dining room, but they work well together, keep up a low, nonstop roar, form a closely knit collective, as we would have said in the Soviet Union. We take some white wine, pile our plates with crackers, cheese, carrot sticks, green onions, radishes, cauliflower, and broccoli, and drift toward the wall where, having secured at least one flank, we hope to munch our harvest in peace.

No sooner do we make contact with the wall, however, than an elegantly dressed, middle-aged gentleman comes up to us and tells us how glad he is to make our acquaintance at last. "You may wonder how I recognized you. It was very simple, actually. I saw a picture of you in a magazine not long ago. A perfect likeness it was too. I even remember your dog. A fine specimen, by the way."

"My dog?" That throws me. There is no doubt in my mind that our little Ushik is a fine specimen, but we have never had our picture in a magazine together. Perhaps our kind American friend was laboring under a false impression?

"Oh no!" he protests. "I remember it well. You had a dog in your lap."

My wife and I call time out and go into a huddle. "I think you once had your picture taken with a book in your lap," she says to me in Russian. "Maybe there was a dog on the cover."

While our interlocutor listens patiently to our foreign speech, an acquaintance of his comes up and he introduces us as those distinguished Dutch visitors . . . "What did you say your name was again?"

We have to disappoint him. "I'm terribly sorry, but I'm Russian, not Dutch."

"But wasn't that Dutch you were speaking to your wife?"

"No, it was Russian. We belong to the same tribe."

"Then why did I take you for Dutch?" He looks awfully puzzled.

"It's perfectly natural. We Russians have a great deal in common with the Dutch. In the first place, neither of us speaks English as a mother tongue, and in the second place, they taught us to build ships."

At that moment a gong rings out from the depths of the living room and our host asks us all for our attention. Suddenly everything falls into place: the guest of honor is a Dutchman, Erasmus Rotterboom, a prizewinning Esso executive. He steps up on a small podium, thanks the host for the introduction, gives a brief talk about his achievements, and launches into a violin recital.

Through it all Maya keeps throwing me sidelong glances. "Yes," I whisper, "it's a remarkable country, Holland. Entirely below sea level, and look at the contribution it's made to civilization: windmills, skates, canals, tulips, trade on the high seas, and now our violinist friend here. Besides, it was Holland that taught our Party Secretary Peter the Great all he knew, including, or so rumor would have it, the art of love. . . . What a shame, really, that Russo-Dutch relations have gone downhill ever since. Why, two hundred fifty years ago Russians made pilgrimages to Holland in much the way Soviets today make pilgrimages to the People's Republic of Hungary."

"That may well be," Maya whispers, "but what has it got to do with the party we were invited to?"

During the following round of applause for Mr. Rotterboom we slip out into O Street. "We must have written the number down wrong," I say. "Look over there at the house with the two small columns and the two winged dogs on the porch. Isn't that good old Rear Admiral T. about to go in? That must be our party."

We walk the hundred yards and go inside. Here the guests are mostly women of what in Russian we call a "Balzacian," that is, mature, age. The very air is redolent with starched lace. We arrive just in time for the main course: a gigot in the finest "vieille cuisine" tradition. I introduce myself to the woman on my right and ask her where to find Mr. and Mrs. Cooper-Clark.

"Just call me Lulu, pal," she says, giving me a clap on the back. "But now that you mention it, I haven't seen the Coop or little Ms. Clarkie all night."

"Don't tell me we're at the wrong party again," I say to Maya, who confesses she has been wondering the same thing. "If it weren't for Rear Admiral T., Greg and Heidi, Mel Dershkowitz, and the Princess Trubetskaya, I'd have hightailed it out of here in a panic."

"You're not thinking of leaving now, are you folks?" asks Lulu.

"No, we'll stick around for a while."

"What's this 'for a while' business?" she says with the coy wink of the boogie-woogie queen she had doubtless once been. "You won't regret it. We're all going skinny-dipping after dinner. By the way, how're things up there in Quebec?"

Trying to picture her in her after-dinner costume, I spy a name tag on her left breast: "Lulu Smiley—*Kiss Me Not Shyly.*" I glance around and see similar name tags on similar breasts: "Doris Garbowski—*Till Death Do Us Part,*" "Nancy Tarantine—*Crossing Mount Destiny,*" Kandi Ambivalenstein—*When the Heart Calls.*"... Had we listened a bit closer to their conversation, we'd have realized straightaway we had happened on a convention of heartthrob romance writers.

We show up at the third party in time for dessert. One waiter is pushing around a pastry cart, another serving liqueurs. Our crowd—Greg and Heidi, Mel Dershkowitz, the Princess Trubetskaya, and Rear Admiral T.—is chopping away at cheesecakes and spooning away mousses even while inching toward the door.

"Missed the boat again!" says the rear admiral, shaking

his graying locks. "Infantry." He is not far off: it turns out to be a reunion of the mountain climbers who have scaled the east side of Kilimanjaro.

"We must have written the *letter* down wrong," I realize at last. "Our party must have been on Q Street, not O Street. It may be the same vicious circle, but at least it has a squiggle for an escape hatch."

Sketches for a Novel to Be

1 9 7 5 /   Sochi. Lyova Groshkin, future Californian, has come to a decision. "I refuse to grow old! It's stupid—giving up youth for age. I just won't let it happen. I'll do anything! Growing old is unfair!"

"Reflexes," he explains to the HMN. "The main thing is reflexes." They are jogging under a banner proclaiming another of Brezhnev's doctrines: THE HEALTH OF EACH IS THE HEALTH OF ALL. "Never give them a chance to deteriorate." Two "Americans" out for their daily jog along the Sochi coast amidst an otherwise solidly, stolidly Soviet crowd. "I won't be here for long, actually," he confesses as they run on. "I'm going to America. In America nobody's old. There's this Professor Sotospeak who married the great-granddaughter of a fellow classmate and had two kids by her."

"How old are you anyway, Lyova?"

"What difference does it make? The only thing that counts is reflexes."

"But what's that gray stuff in your beard?"

Bull's-eye. Lyova's whole face puckers in displeasure—and immediately looks the older for it. But he soon takes himself in hand and smiles a toothy, youthful grin. "Can't give you any dope on the beard. I've never seen it. But it's still nice and thick. I can feel that."

"Are you at home in English?" the HMN asks in at-home English.

"English? Who needs it?"

1 9 8 0 / General Pxi, the man in charge of air-conditioning at the Pacifist Palisades, regards the manager of the condominium, Bernadette Luxe, as a Greenland of a woman, and contrives whenever possible to tag along in the shade of her monumental proportions. In his eyes she transcends the physical and enters the realm of the symbolic. Her body is a nuclear freeze wafting up out of stairwells and through halls, her slopes glitter gold like glaciers beneath the evening sun, her pendulous mammary glands burn his tiny hands like ice. "Justa cooling off," he says as he weighs them. "Justa cooling off." General Pxi belongs to the international generation of the "burned" and is in constant need of refrigeration.

Randolph Golenzo, pipe in teeth, observes their interaction from the deck and wonders why such harmony was so difficult to come by on the battlefield.

1 9 8 0 / In an all-night Westwood Boulevard boutique you can buy a Lenin T-shirt with his nibs smiling out at you from a Kazan University insignia. Once more, like a nagging toothache, the question returns: Why did the young man drop out of his alma mater? You might ask the T-shirt salesman. But all he'll do is wink and say, "Sorry, we're still new at the game."

5 Once we had decided to settle on the shores of the Potomac, we began looking for a place even closer to the center of things. For the apartment rents charged by rapacious District landlords you can get a whole house on the other side of the river in Virginia or Maryland, but the American taste for suburban life was still alien to us. We were drawn to the Parisian-like cafés and bookshops of Dupont Circle.

"How can you move downtown?" friends warned us. "It's so dangerous." But the Silver Spring house of one of them had been burglarized twice that year. The first time the thieves took the silverware, the second time the television set; neither time did they touch the priceless sixteenth-century Russian icons. Did our friends think the District attracted more sophisticated thieves?

Apartment hunting brings home, so to speak, the duality of émigré existence: you want something that reminds you of your former life yet something you did not have—could not have had—in that life. Responding to an ad in the papers for a Wyoming Avenue apartment on the mild slopes of the city's only hill, we realized immediately we had found what we were looking for. A white-walled duplex complete with spiral staircase and view of the Capitol, the Washington Monument, and the colonnade of the Lincoln Memorial, it could not have existed in Moscow and evoked the vague visions of our Muscovite dreams.

For this smashing pad on the border between Dupont Circle and the popular Adams Morgan section of town we agreed to pay what at the time seemed a fortune: $1200 a month. At the black market exchange rate that comes to 4800 rubles, two years of wages; at the official rate—six months of wages. (Recall the comparative prices of the Soviet and American tanks.)

The manager was a young man of the yuppie tribe, a Mr. Brik. (We later learned that he was of Lithuanian descent and that his ancestral name was something like Olbrikaus-kauskas.) "I must show you one thing," he said, ushering us into the lobby. "It may amaze you at first, but in time, take my word for it, it will simplify your life enormously."

"What could this marvel be?" we wondered as we filed past the mailboxes and stopped at the elevator doors. "Here, look," he said. "A button. All you have to do is push it"—he pushed it—"and soon these doors will open"—they opened. "You may enter without fear." We walked into the elevator. "On this panel you see two rows of buttons. Each button has a number on it. The number corresponds to a floor. Push the bottom button"—he pushed it—"and the doors will close"—they closed. "Don't panic now. The cabin will deliver you safely to the floor of your choice, where the doors will open automatically"—they did. "When you want to go down, all you have to do is repeat the procedure in reverse. That's not too complicated, now, is it?"

We waited until he had finished, then responded in our best American, "Come off it, Dave! You don't really believe there are no elevators in Russia, do you?"

Mr. Olbrikauskauskas was crestfallen. A Russia with elevators? We had destroyed an image, a whole system of images. After that he pointed out the apartment's techno-logical extras like an actor throwing away his lines: "Oh yes, and here's a doohickey—but you know about that—and there's the dingus—though I'm sure they're better in Russia." Actually, most of the things we had only read about in Russia, if that—things like thermostats, a built-in washer and drier, a dishwasher, a microwave oven, a self-cleaning oven (we still haven't figured out the timing device), an exhaust system, a sink disposal unit, and finally a compactor. When we mumbled something about bourgeois decadence, Mr. Brik came back with, "Don't worry. You're in America now."

I digress from my homely descriptions to cast a glance at our technological civilization. Our every step, our every move is tied to technology. Our white Wyoming cube is stuffed with it, piled high with cassettes, records, the upstairs tape recorder, radio, TV set, the downstairs tape recorder, radio, TV set, a VCR, a single lens reflex, a Polaroid, four typewriters (three electric, one electronic), a PC and printer, a copy machine, several calculators, a baby Benz under the living-room window and the old Omega out in the street, not to mention the Exercycle, shower massage, electric hair drier, electric shaver, electric blanket, electric hair curlers, electric coffee grinder, coffee maker, food processor, toaster, iron, vacuum cleaner . . . And that is only half of what surrounds us (two Russian émigrés getting on in years and a sprightly cocker spaniel) every minute of the day.

Is there an end to it all? Setting aside the various possible apocalyptic predictions (a necessary though not particularly urgent element of civilization), let us pose a more modest question: have we come to a dead end? When I hear people complaining that America has slowed down or ground to a halt, I can't help wondering whether there's anywhere left to go. Now that capitalism has brought luxury to the millions, it has reached a certain plateau. If it intends to develop, it must branch out in other directions— work to improve mass taste, for instance.

Even at its present stage, however, capitalism exhibits concentrated pockets of features justly deplored by Marx. Take our alley, that is, the view from our back windows (the ones that don't look out on the Capitol). Every day at 6:00 A.M. we witness the rivalry of four trash-removal companies (my favorite boasts the surname of a once-celebrated French poet and Lenin Peace Prize laureate—Aragon Waste); one after the other, four huge trucks fill the alley with the din of early capitalism. For all its Mercedeses, BMWs, Jaguars, and Corvettes it has a shabby, run-down quality about it; it is always muddy and full of ruts.

The alley has another eyesore as well: a spooky shack with a roof of bumpy pitch and tufts of wild grass. The cellar is intermittently inhabited by a group of multiracial bums who arrive in the middle of the night in a Rolls-Royce. The trash sometimes piles up five or six feet high because the owner of the restaurant next door—we suspect him of Socialist leanings—refuses to participate in the trash competition: he feels *his* waste should be removed by the public sanitation force. (The public sanitation force obviously adheres to a different point of view.) Who should see to the rats in the cellar appears a moot question.

At first we refused to believe our eyes. Hefty rats running around the capital of the United States of America? No, they must be pets of some kind—giant gerbils, perhaps. Then we found a dead "gerbil" next to our car. A rat, no two ways about it. We ran to our neighbors, a clean-cut yuppie couple, who shrugged and said, "Big deal. A rat. Forget it"; we ran to the block captain, who promised to work on the capitalist Socialist, and although the trash disappeared (Aragon apparently won the Augean stables contract), the rats did not. In the Soviet Union the situation would have been declared an emergency by the municipal department of epidemiology, but in America no one appears particularly put out.

And the cockroaches! When Yevgeny Yevtushenko discovered a dozen of the little bastards in his Moscow apartment, he shot off a poem entitled "Cockroaches in a High Rise." Since the Russian mind characterizes both cockroaches and Stalin by their "mustaches," the poem was read as an act of civic courage. The association does not seem to hold in America.

When an upright Soviet citizen discovers something untoward going on, he rants and raves and shouts "How is this possible under socialism?" In America no one would ever dream of shouting "How is that possible under capitalism?" No one but a Soviet émigré, that is.

For us, capitalism is modern technology, efficient service, and sound fiscal policy, whereas socialism is outdated technology, rudeness, and primary market relations of the "you scratch my back, I'll scratch yours" variety: favor for favor, commodity for commodity, commodity for favor, favor for commodity. Anything to get by. But while the USSR inches toward capitalism, capitalism, the Russian émigré discovers to his dismay, is undergoing a Socialist warp of apathy, poor service, and hackwork.

Maya takes a jacket to the tailor. Nothing complicated: the sleeves need a little shortening. "Ten days," says the woman behind the counter, without looking up from her MTV. Ten days to shorten sleeves? Hmm. In the Soviet Union you give the woman an extra three rubles and your coat is ready in an hour. That doesn't seem to work here. And not only that. When Maya returns ten days later, the woman can't even find the jacket. Her response to Maya's indignation? A mocking grin: she is protected by her union.

The sink disposal unit goes on the blink. The management promises to send a plumber. The plumber shows up—a week later. In the Soviet Union you call in a man, whose name always seems to be Nikolai, and for five rubles in cash he takes care of anything that needs taking care of.

For six months the little cabin that was meant to make our lives so easy was out of service because of a dispute between the elevator company and the building co-op; for six months we struggled up four flights of stairs with our packages. When an elevator breaks down in Moscow, the co-op shareholders chip in and grease the palm of Nikolai the Second. Is that socialism or capitalism?

Shortly after moving in, we had a marvelous experience

with a local department store or, rather, with its furniture department or, to be even more precise, with its furniture delivery department. We had bought a glass and steel table, half a dozen chairs, and an armchair, and were promised delivery in two weeks. Two weeks! In the Soviet Union you find the department store Nikolai, grease his palm, and the furniture arrives, under his personal escort, the following morning.

Maybe because that doesn't seem to work here, we had to wait three weeks instead of two, but on the morning of the first day of the third week "Mr. Eskintow" received a phone call requesting him not to leave the house between nine and five. The furniture was coming! Hurray!

Our joy was premature: the furniture did not arrive on that day or the next or during the next few weeks. In response to my calls the operator invariably asked, "What is your name, please?" and "How do you spell it?" and then passed us to another woman who would ask whether "that was S as in soup" and "V as in vase," only to fob me off on a real featherbrain, who asked me to start from scratch: "A as in air. K as in kite. S as in soup. Y as in young. O as in office. N as in new. O as in office again. V as in vase."

The fifth time I phoned—at the end of each previous call I had been told soothingly, "It's in process"—I spelled my name: "A as in anapest, K as in kibitzer, S as in surrealism, Y as in Yoknapatawpha, O as in orgasm, N as in nepotism, O as in orgasm again, V as in ventriloquism."

Silence. "Are you with me?" I asked tactfully.

"Yes sir," muttered an uncertain voice.

"By the way, what's *your* name?"

"Nancy Roosevelt."

"Is that R as in renaissance, O as in . . ."

She hung up.

The next day, that is, a full month and a half after our purchase, the furniture arrived. True, the armchair had no casters and the chairs were from different families, but the table seemed all right. "I've got nothing to do with it," said

the deliveryman. "Talk to the company. I just work there."
But we thought we discerned a certain look in his eye.
Despite certain differences in race there was something of
the Nikolai about him. Had the time come for America to
return to primary relations?

ADAMS MORGAN: A BABY BABYLON IN GREATER ATHENS

Also shortly after we moved in, an elderly man in a Burberry knocked at the door, introduced himself as Ray
Burns, the block captain, and welcomed us to Wyoming. I
see him every day now. He's always busy with some project—mowing the lawn, planting flowers, picking up broken
glass. No one pays him a penny for it.

Incidentally, broken bottles are a great American mys-
tery to me. I have never witnessed a bottle actually being
broken, yet I find splinters of glass everywhere I look. One
of the multitudinous differences between Russians and
Americans is that Russians return bottles, Americans
smash them. And Mr. Burns gathers up the shards with an
understanding smile. People like him, of old Scots-Irish
stock, form the commonsense backbone of the country and
its patchwork population.

That first day Mr. Burns presented us with a copy of the
block newsletter, handwritten in Mrs. Burns's fine hand
and photocopied. It began with wishes for a Merry Christ-
mas and a Happy New Year. Then Sergeant Jerry Krieger
from the Third Police Precinct called on the residents to
join the battle against crime. The statistics for Wyoming
Avenue for the past six months had been pretty good: one
robbery and some minor items taken from parked cars. The
precinct's department of social services announced it had
handed out twenty-five holiday baskets to needy families.

Next Mr. Burns reported on a chat he had had with Mrs.
Claire Sizer, who moved to Wyoming Avenue in the thir-

ties. The whole thing bore an uncanny similarity to Docto-
row's *Ragtime*, which I had translated while still in the Soviet Union. It ran something like this: "The houses on our
block were built between 1910 and 1920, and the neighborhood has always enjoyed an *excellent reputation* thanks to its
fine location and outstanding residents. Dr. Stiles, Calvin
Coolidge's personal physician (he treated President Coolidge's youngest son for blood poisoning until the young-
ster's tragic demise), used to live here, as did—just
think!—Commodore Robert E. Peary, the man who conquered the North Pole." Mr. Burns sticks so close to *Ragtime* that he places one of the book's heroes on Wyoming.
"Mrs. Sizer," he goes on, "is still a sweet and sprightly lady
at the age of ninety-two. 'I would not wish to live anywhere
but in Washington,' she says. 'I was born here, and come
what may I love the place.' "

The newsletter concludes with a debate on the problem
of one-way traffic, a notice from the local community center, an item about volunteer crocus and daffodil plantings,
and an ad for a neighbor who sells figurines—elephants,
ducks, and owls—made from seashells.

Wyoming Avenue, which consists primarily of three-
story Victorian houses and has only two commercial enterprises (an all-night 7-Eleven for physical sustenance and a
shop specializing in occult books and objects for more
spiritual needs), may be considered part of three neighborhoods—diplomatic Kalorama, aristocratic Dupont Circle,
and ethnic Adams Morgan. Adams Morgan, which owes its
name to two early desegregated schools, styles itself a miniature New York, which, fortunately for those of us who live
there, is something of an exaggeration. New York still lacks
the chutzpah to style itself an overgrown Adams Morgan.

If we do resemble New York, it is in the motley splendor
of our citizenry. At the Saturday market (at Eighteenth
Street and Columbia Road) you'll see just about everyone:
local truck farmers, Frenchmen, Koreans, Chinese, Viet-

namese, Indians, Arabs, Latin Americans, American blacks, Caribbean blacks, and large numbers of Africans, especially the gentle Nigerians. Once my wife told a black saleswoman that we had a holiday coming up: Orthodox Easter. The saleswoman beamed and said, "I'm Orthodox too. I'm a refugee from Colonel Mengistu's regime in Ethiopia."

Not surprisingly Adams Morgan is a hotbed of political variety. Passing Revolutionary Books the other day, I recalled a recent *Literaturnaya gazeta* article about "raging reactionaries in America." The McCarthy era was back, the author informed his readers. If an American reads a forbidden book, if he even so much as receives a letter from the camp of peace and socialism, he will immediately end up—oh, how I love those clichés!—filling the ranks of the unemployed; he may even land in jail. The Reagan administration has closed the gates to all sources of truthful information: it monitors the sale of shortwave radios and has banned *Literaturnaya gazeta* from the newsstands!

On a hunch I went into the bookshop. "What books by Trotsky have you got in stock?" I asked the two young salesmen, who were sitting under a life-size, full-length poster of Lenin in cap and a red bow on the lapel of his jacket.

"Well . . ." said one, hesitantly.

"Actually . . ." said the other, playing for time.

"You see, Trotsky's view of the revolution was rather one-sided," said the first.

"But we do have an excellent study by a professor at Havana University," said the second, perking up. "Here it is. *The Vicious Essence of Trotskyism.*"

"Not today, thank you," I said, "but perhaps you can help me with something else." I pointed to the portraits of men like Stalin, Brezhnev, Mao Tse-tung, and Ho Chi Minh. "Which do you think is most attractive?"

"In what way?" they asked, confused.

"Well, in terms of male beauty."

They exchanged a look, frowned, and said disapprovingly, "An irrelevant issue . . ."

"One last request. Have you got something by Marshal Lavrenty Beria?"

This time the joke was on me. I was immediately offered *On the History of Bolshevist Organization in the Transcaucasus* in a translation that brought across the author's Georgian accent with great verve.

Reactionary forces may have taken over in *some* neighborhoods, but in Adams Morgan, Stalin's minister of internal affairs is alive and well and the revolution lives!

Adams Morgan is also a haven for street people. Although American English has many words for them—"tramp," "bum," "hobo"—we like to think of them as our own version of the French *clochard* or Soviet Russian *bich* (which, believe it or not, comes from the English word "beach" and apparently derives from the idea that a *bich* would rather be lolling on the beach than toiling away at sea). Since, as I learned at a block party, so many of my neighbors are writers, I suspect some of the *bichi* of having retired prematurely from the profession. One of them always asks me for five dollars. It's the kind of reverse largesse you'd expect from a writer.

Sketches for a Novel to Be

1 9 8 o–8 1 / On his days off, the HMN doesn't look a thing like a parking attendant for the El Greco. When the occasion calls for a suit, he slips on his Ted Lapidus; when the occasion calls for a raincoat, he slips on his Burberry; when the occasion calls for dress shoes, he slips on his Churches. It never occurs to anyone he's picked them up secondhand. "The ultimate fashion plate," they think. "Always at home in comfortable classics."

Now we see him approaching St. Matthew's Cathedral under the watchful eye of a handsome beggar in his late thirties whose trademarks include a pair of bare, suppurating feet and a mop of red curls held in place by a leather band. I call him a beggar, but perhaps he is nothing more than an aging hippie. In any case, accosting the HMN with a dignity even Bob Dylan would envy, he says, "Brother, can you spare a buck?"

Ah, inflation, thinks the HMN as he reaches for his well-worn Christian Dior wallet.

"Thanks," says the surprised beggar as he reaches for the dollar bill. "I was skeptical about you."

"How come?" our hero replies with a shrug of the shoulders. "What's a buck between beggars? Haven't you ever heard of solidarity?"

1 9 8 2 / Randy Golenzo is celebrating his recent promotion with a bash in the "hereditary town home." He's laid

in a supply of ground round and hasn't forgotten to put out the A.1 sauce or warn the relatives that "there'll be a few of those Palisades kooks aboard."

And sure enough, get a load of those three! Bernadette the Magnificent and her plunging neckline immediately strike a Greco-Roman note. General Pxi, sporting his best khaki tunic (medal-festooned, of course) and a spanking new *Playboy* bunny, undertakes an inspection of the Golenzo residence air-conditioning system and immediately starts shaking his well-groomed head and muttering, "To think we counted on your infrastructure!" And who should the third man turn out to be but the ex-Russian jogger Lyova Groshkin, whom Bernadette has recently picked up at her rollerskating lessons in Santa Melinda.

Lyova is flourishing in America. With a part-time job as a furniture mover for Starving Students and a little help from the welfare people, he has no trouble sticking to his 120-mile-a-week jogging regime, and the friendship with Bernadette Luxe has added a new harmony to his circulatory system. Combining it all with a scientifically controlled diet and regular reflex checkups, he has managed to reverse the aging process; in other words, he now looks half his fifty years—at least to those who did not know him back when. As for those who did, he does his best to avoid them. "The old fogeys," he calls them with understandable scorn.

Whenever Lyova was introduced to the local population, he introduced himself as "Champion." Since Russian uses the English word, he could use the Russian, and it got him off to a flying start. "Be nice to Mr. Golenzo, will you, Champ?" Bernadette says to him. "He's got connections."

Lyova nods. Nodding is easy. Although he knew not a word of English, he had a good imagination. He could also make his wants known well enough. *"Gamburgery!"* he shouts in Russian, and before he can shake a stick at one he is munching away.

Randy clearly likes the way Lyova handles himself. "You think those are hamburgers, do you?" he says with a smile. "Here, try a little A.1 sauce on it, and you'll have a real steakburger."

His nephew Jason grabs the enormously thick concoction out of his hands and—can a little squirt like that really open his mouth so wide? "Hey, wait a second! That's your Uncle Randy's steakburger," Golenzo shouts, grabbing it back while everyone has a good chuckle.

"Stateburger," Lyova muses. "Hey, Bernadette wasn't kidding. This guy must really be well connected."

6 Tired yet proud, I delivered a thick packet of papers to the Immigration and Naturalization Service: I had completed the paperwork for a green card and the right to permanent residency in the United States of America. It was my fifth visit to the office. This time, though, I was certain everything was shipshape, all tied up and looking pretty. Any immigrant will understand my pride and my exhaustion: the moment in question represents the culmination of round after round in the dismal bureaucratic rigmarole that Americans eloquently call, to the amusement of Soviet and Soviet-bloc émigrés, red tape.

It all started in Los Angeles. When we heard I had been deprived of Soviet citizenship, I naturally applied for political asylum. We went to the Los Angeles Immigration and Naturalization Service and completed the forms, and after waiting more than a year for them to follow us to Washington, we were informed that the Los Angeles INS had . . . lost them. The irony of it all (and irony seems to follow us wherever we go) is that I had come to Washington to write a novel about a Soviet citizen floundering in the waves of a paper sea.

In any case, we started over from scratch, this time in Washington, and once we had received "refugee" papers (which, for example, gave us the right to travel outside the country—and return), we were ready for the next step: permanent residency.

Our visits to E Street were spaced out over a year. Each

time we waited several hours in a line of our brothers-in-exile; each time we presented our papers to an INS official; each time we were turned away empty-handed. There was always something missing or something not quite in order: one or another medical form had been completed incorrectly or at the wrong hospital, and so on and so forth. But at last there was nothing left to cavil at. We had surmounted all obstacles. We had reached perfection. We had constructed a bureaucratic chef d'oeuvre.

Or had we? we couldn't help worrying as the day of our appointment came near. All my life I've been unlucky in affairs of the bureaucracy. I never seem to get through without some kind of hitch or misunderstanding, be it only a misprint. *There* I could put it down to *their* damned system; *here* I could only wait and wonder.

When a friend advised me to supplement my file with articles published in the American press about me and my books, I was a bit disconcerted: I didn't want to toot my own horn, after all. "You don't understand the American way," he told me. "You're crazy not to take advantage of all *positive information!*"

The first thing the INS woman did when we got in to see her (after duly shuffling through the line, that is) was to lay the "positive information" aside without even glancing at it. Then she delved into the juicy pile of papers (not without a certain concupiscence, or so it seemed to me), peering up at me from time to time without, to put it mildly, the slightest hint of encouragement. She was an attractive black woman with large golden earrings.

"Where is your FUR-1980-X-551?" she asked impassively, but I had the impression deep down she was having trouble subduing an anti-Aksyonov volcanic hostility of a vehemence to burn through even the high-quality leather of my Oxfords.

The form she asked for was not on the required list. None of her colleagues had mentioned it: when they needed the information it provided, they accessed it on their computers. Feeling I was about to go down yet again, but still thrashing to keep afloat, I pointed out to her obligingly that the information called for in FUR-1980-X-551 was available on line.

"Are you trying to teach me my job?" Her voice was like an emery board against my skin; it immediately conjured up her Soviet bureau-bitch counterparts. But there was something new in it as well, something unfamiliar.

When she tossed the file back at me and told me through her teeth that I would have to go to another office to clarify certain details (in other words, that I would have to go back to square one again), I had no time to think through what made her react so negatively to me; I simply tried to save the day by mumbling something else about the computer and never having been asked for the form before. Then suddenly the suppressed volcano did erupt, and a veritable Krakatoa it was too. "Not another word!" she roared. "Not another word, do you hear? You have no rights in this country! You're a refugee! The United States government did not ask you to live here!"

I never expected to come across anything like that in America, nor had I in fact come across anything even approximating it. True, I had been here long enough to learn that America has its own thriving brand of bureaucracy (which, in contrast to the decrepit conscience-ridden Soviet brand, is complacent and self-satisfied), but until that blow-up it had always been on its best behavior; it was correct in the way a computer is correct, a computer that has not yet had boorishness programmed into it.

Actually, "boorishness" does not quite bring across the Russian word I have in mind. That word is *khamstvo,* and the quality it denotes goes further and deeper than "boorish" or "loutish," the standard Russian-English dictionary translations (just as the standard English-Russian dictionary translations of the English word *privacy* do not quite capture the concept behind it).

In any case, language differences got me into even

deeper trouble with my Krakatoa. I began my response to her tirade with the words "I don't think you heard what I said, *lady* . . ." What I had thought to be a perfectly polite word—a gracious word, in fact, the equivalent of the French *madame*—turned out in this context to be hideously out of place.

"If you find us so hard to deal with," she countered, jumping up from behind her desk, "you can just pack up and leave the country!"

There was a dramatic pause while we stood glaring at each other. Her eyes were full of—well, if not hate, then some highly inflammable formula. What had I done to provoke such violent emotion in her? I had clearly misused the word "lady," but was that enough to provoke rage?

"Can't you see?" said a Polish refugee who happened to be at the INS that day. "It's racial. Racial hatred."

"But we had a black woman taking care of us before her, and she was fine."

"Well, not all whites are racists either. You're not, now, are you?"

No, I am not a racist and never have been. But then I'd never considered the possibility of being the *object* of racism. Because I am white, I took it for granted that I was immune, that no one could be prejudiced against me. In other words, I too—unconsciously, at least—was influenced by racist stereotypes: I assumed, on the one hand, that only a white could be a racist and, on the other, that a white could never be the object of racial hatred, to say nothing of its victim. Even though I had come from a country where racism is not so burning an issue as it is in America, I must still exhibit certain "white man's complexes" and perhaps a certain condescension in dealing with my black brothers. But is that racism?

My friend the Pole had some well-developed opinions on the subject: "People of our background, refugees from Eastern Europe, are in a rather ambiguous position here. We look like the majority, but our accents and cultural reflexes relegate us to minority status. Besides, our feelings of alienation from and condescension to the blacks are stronger than those of Americans, who have lived side by side with them for generations. And don't think the blacks can't sense it. You go into that room and, accent or no accent, you're white and your wife is blond; *ergo,* you belong to the dominant race. No matter how you behave you can be suspected of arrogance on the one hand or condescension on the other. Even if you go so far as to demean yourself, she'll think, *'They* don't find it demeaning to demean themselves in front of *us.'* Now I want you to be absolutely honest. What were your innermost thoughts as you stood there glaring at her?"

"I just thought, 'The bureaucratic bitch!' and, well, compared her to the Soviet variety. There were no racial overtones at all."

"Remember, now. Your *innermost* thoughts."

I scratched my head. "I don't know. I guess I could have thought something like, 'Wouldn't you know that we'd get a black official . . .'"

"There, you see? Bureaucracy is only part of the story."

Merely by throwing in our lot with America, we play a part in her race relations—we and all the other émigrés of the "Caucasian" race. Walk along the street, and you're part of the racial landscape.

One of my black friends (and unfortunately, though I live in a city where 70 percent of the population is black, I can count those black friends on my fingers) has explained the ambiguity of our position to me from his point of view. "I was born in this country," he said, "as were my parents and their parents before them. Our African progenitor goes back so far I can't trace him. And you? You're a foreigner. Open your mouth and everybody hears an accent. But ten years from now that accent will have improved and you'll more or less become *one of them.* I can never be *one of them.* The first thing they think when they see me is 'He's black';

only then do they notice how I'm dressed, what mood I'm in—who I am. The syndrome is even more pronounced than usual in my case because I'm *very* black. That's right: even the degree of pigmentation enters into it." My friend is in fact very black.

"But you have no reason to complain," I pointed out. "After all, you're a prosperous lawyer, you own a beautiful house in the District, you drive a Mercedes 450, you don't seem to lack female company, black or white . . ."

He smiled, and his face lit up like a flashlight. "Yes, my shade is quite acceptable, I suppose, though the blacks with the greatest social success are the ones who are all but white, the ones who are called 'high yellow' and look like whites after a Florida holiday."

"But I repeat: you seem to have no reason to complain."

"And I'm *not* complaining. What I have in mind is something much more subtle than oppression or even prejudice; what I have in mind will probably go on for a good two hundred years: it's called alienation."

Even though we do our best on this terribly complicated subject to *analyze* all the niceties and not-so-niceties of the situation, we really do little more than *experience* them. And in a city like Washington we can't help experiencing them, and on a day-to-day basis. Sometimes we see the lighter side of things; sometimes we see their strange, sad, twisted, absurd side; sometimes we smell the poisonous fumes.

Robert Kaiser, an old friend who is an editor of the *Washington Post,* has told us of how, in his lifetime, Negroes were not allowed to occupy orchestra seats in Washington theaters. Inconceivable as that sort of humiliation seems today in a city where not only the majority of the population but also the mayor is black, a large segment of the population still remembers it vividly.

Of all the groups that migrated to the New World, only the blacks left the Old World under duress. But then—and this may sound blasphemous to some—it was the slave traders and their dirty business which, through one of history's great ironies, led to the founding of the American black community, and it has to be said that the progress the American black community has made surpasses that of any African nation.

Notice I say "African *nation*" but "American black *community.*" We who come from a multinational country, the Union of Soviet Socialist Republics, need some time to adjust to the idea that this literally is "one nation indivisible." Just as whites trace their roots to various European ethnic groups, so blacks trace their roots to various African ethnic groups, but the nation all the groups have formed here is one.

In the Soviet Union we were taught otherwise. From early childhood we were saturated with clichés about the Negro race as the emblem of imperialist oppression, the Negro as the epitome of international solidarity and sympathy—anything but the Negro as human being. Later, when people began to question what official sources told them, there were those who concluded that racism was not an issue in the United States, that it had been fabricated, like so much else, by the Soviet propaganda machine.

But whether my generation in Russia considered Americans prejudiced or not, we went wild over black jazz musicians and black athletes and were therefore convinced we hadn't a drop of prejudice in us. As soon as we set foot in America, however, we realized we were often more prejudiced than the locals. Not that we harbored negative feelings toward the blacks. On the contrary. *Our* racism was a racism of *positive* feelings: we balked at any sharp comment or criticism directed against them. It took us awhile to realize that the blacks can do very well without our condescension, thank you. Maybe the Brighton Beach crowd, lately of Odessa, had the right idea when they told the black hoods of Brooklyn, "Listen, guys, we're not the ones who sold your forefathers into slavery, so lay off, will you?"

Duplicitous amiability, if I may call it that, is what leads "fine, upstanding people" (people who think of others as prejudiced if they complain of blacks, say, breaking a law) to speak of a neighborhood that "is changing" or "has gone downhill" when what they mean is simply that blacks have moved in. There is, of course, nothing at all "progressive" in this kind of amiability, and blacks are rightly outraged by it. But what is wrong with saying that in search of an easy high the Russians and the Irish produce more than their share of drunkards? What is wrong with saying that in search of an easy high black youths do more than their share of damage?

The black community has faces as varied as any other: a fine young athlete like the Olympic champion Carl Lewis and the psychopath detective who killed the father of a Russian émigré family in New York for no apparent reason; Mayor Tom Bradley of Los Angeles and the Black Muslim Nazi Louis Farrakhan; my artist friends next door and the Washington INS official I locked horns with. One way or another, they are all our new fellow citizens.

SOVIET BLACKS

How did the Soviet image of the Negro take shape? In 1937, at the height of Stalin's purges, the Soviet film director Grigory Alexandrov came up with a stylish musical comedy called *The Circus*. Somewhere behind the gags, special effects, and fancy dancing was the melodramatic story of an American vaudeville star who in racist America manages to give birth to a black baby. The film opens with a swarm of virulent racists chasing after the train that carries away our heroine, a dazzling blonde whom no Hollywood studio would have failed to sign up. (Her name, by the way, was Lyubov Orlova.) While on tour in Moscow, she falls in love with a Soviet actor, but hides her Negro baby from him out of shame. As time goes on, however, she realizes that in the Soviet Union everyone is equal, everyone is free, and the film ends with her singing "I have never seen a country where the people breathe so easy" while her little black baby is passed through the circus audience from beaming Soviet citizen to beaming Soviet citizen, each of whom happens to represent another of the country's many minority groups.

Incidentally, the baby needed no blackface. He was played by Jim Patterson, the newly born son of an American Communist couple, both of whom were black. Patterson had the most privileged of childhoods; he even went to Artek, the Pioneer camp in the Crimea reserved for the offspring of the biggest party wigs. He grew up to become a Soviet poet, a less than mediocre one unfortunately.

The postwar need for black actors could be met on a more local basis. In the northern port of Arkhangelsk, the gateway to a number of Allied vessels, a full 5 percent of the babies born during the hostilities were black. One of them played the part of a black deckhand on a battleship in a film called *Maxim,* which is meant to show how internationally minded and sympathetic to the oppressed masses the Russian people are.

A popular young Moscow actor in the sixties was quite black, the picture of negritude, in fact. His name was Gely Konovalov, he was born to a Russian family, and he knew no language other than Russian, but he took advantage of his appearance to give poetry readings in a strange, outlandish accent. All doors were open to him; everyone treated him with kid gloves—no one wished to insult a "representative of the oppressed masses" after all. To see him as he really was, you had to catch him at the Theater Society's restaurant in a state approaching inebriation, the only time he seemed able to shake the need to pander to the Soviets' topsy-turvy brand of racism. His fellow actors, who knew from daily makeup sessions that skin color was skin deep, never paid the slightest attention to his complexion.

Primed by the demagoguery of "internationalism," of

propaganda in a variety of media, and of black individuals like the bass Paul Robeson, a famous "friend of the Soviet Union," Soviet consciousness has maintained a clear-cut stereotype of the black from the twenties to the present. A black cannot be evil or clever or perfidious; a black can be only *oppressed*. Even the CTS (our "critically thinking Soviet" from Chapter Two) took this stereotype with him when he emigrated to the States, and he carried it around until reality the rug beater knocked it out of him.

The streaming pedestrian traffic along Fifth Avenue is likely to consist of peaceful, shoulder-to-shoulder ranks of a Filipino and a Hindu and an Eskimo and a Moor and an Aztec and a Greek and a Phoenician and a Persian and an Assyrian and a Gaul and a Celt and a Scythian and a Pecheneg and a Roman and a Carthaginian and, as the poet says, "a proud son of the Slavs and now a Finn and then a wild Tungus and a Kalmyk, the steppes' true friend." Nor would I be surprised to find a few assorted Amazons, centaurs, or denizens of Atlantis . . .

Even though Soviet émigrés may not differ in complexion from the majority of the population, they represent a phenomenon as alien to the American scene as, say, a contingent of Trojans. Moreover, they cling to their dogmas with as much tenacity as New Guinean idol worshipers.

Take the infamous nationality issue. As schoolchildren we had Lenin's "nationality policy" and its principles of internationalism and the equality of nations stuffed down our throats while being systematically deprived of all opportunity to meet and interact with members of other nations. (The only nationalities we did know were the *intra*national Soviet ones covered in the infamous "point number five" of our identity papers.) What was proclaimed as internationalism was actually isolationism laced with a series of preposterous clichés about "liberation struggles" and the "evils of colonialism."

The rickshaw man, for example. He dogged our footsteps from as far back as we can remember, that spindle-shanked, stoop-shouldered representative of the Asian masses, straining under the load of his overfed imperialist. (The imperialist invariably smoked a cigar and rested a sturdy shoe on the poor yellow man's back.) Although such clichés eventually became the butt of ridicule, they left their mark. If they hadn't, I wouldn't have been so surprised by the first real-life rickshaw men I saw.

It was at Waikiki Beach, Honolulu. There they were—strapping young men and women with sunscreen-ad skin and toothpaste-ad smiles, the finest specimens America's universities have to offer—energetically pedaling pedicabs full of Japanese tourists along Kalakaua. The cliché had been turned completely inside out.

America does not *proclaim* its "internationalism"; it simply lets in crowds of exotic foreigners. One winter night we were driving through Maine when what should we see nestled up in the snowy hills but a Polynesian restaurant. America is the perfect example of a non-Leninist nationality policy: the chance to see how various people eat, pray, work, and let their hair down.

In the Soviet Union it has always been commonly assumed that decadent Western civilization is the source of evil—sexual perversion, drugs and other depravities. Not that people were disgusted by the prospect; quite the contrary. Along with the availability of consumer goods, these were considered main attractions of the West. Ironic clichés abound, along the lines of "Ah, the West! What elegant disintegration." When Soviets imagine the West, they think of sex shops with plastic genitalia, nonstop porno flicks, prostitutes of both sexes, and nightclubs jammed with beautiful people sky high on dope.

After a few years in this decadence, I have an amendment—a major source of Western sin is actually the third world, which Soviet ideologues would have us believe is an innocent victim. The third world exports a fair quotient of masterbatory musical rhythms, herbs and powders that twist the mind—in short, the desire to get and stay high at any price.

The idea that Western civilization inevitably involves a drop a moral standards is simply untrue. The West, and especially its Anglo-Saxon variant, represents a last fortress of common sense—a fortress subjected to waves of primitive hedonism from less advanced societies. These are channeled into subcultures like show business and sex business, showing that the West even tries to put order in those omniverous passions.

This said I have no desire to denigrate the work of individuals from the third world furthering the enlightenment and well-being of their peoples. They need no condescension or arrogant permissiveness from outsiders. These people, in fact, are the least likely to blame Western civilization for their problems. Only two of the three worlds—the first and third—maintain real relations with each other. For the second world—the one of the Soviets—the third world is little more than a testing ground for Marxism-Leninism.

Sketches for a Novel to Be

1 9 8 2 / Bernadette Luxe pushed off from the Longevity Center and skated forth into the ocean breeze, her hair trailing behind her like the tail of the famous horse Bucephalus, whose memoirs had been languishing by her bedside for more than a week now. There was nary a trace of the once lethargic condo manager in the present Jane Fonda clone: aerobics had turned her into an eternal nymph and real estate agent. She was accompanied by a fellow agent, Randolph Golenzo by name, who had long since traded his beer belly for a young man's he-man's chest. Proud and free and with the latest in sound systems on their heads, they glided along to the rhythms of Mr. Beethoven's Eroica.

"I've made up my mind," said Bernadette, "and the answer is yes."

"Hey, let's go to my place," said Golenzo, scarcely able to contain his joy. "I have Better Choice for better ideas."

Thus it was that a new phenomenon, a whole new stratum of society, was born, one which now goes by the name of yuppiedom.

And who should jog rhythmically onto the horizon at just that point but—need I say more?—Lyova Groshkin and General Pxi.

1 9 8 3 / To support his get-young-quick habit, Lyova Groshkin found a three-night-a-week job as doorman at a

thriving restaurant known as the Nouveau Riche. He would glue an outrageous pair of mustachios on his upper lip and claim to be a Serb prince, Tito's personal physician during the Partisan resistance movement, and although his story made not a whit of political or historical sense, no one seemed to care, perhaps because the Nouveau Riche regulars had as much trouble with English as he had or because the Nouveau Riche regulars were themselves never quite what they claimed to be.

7 Perched in the flag tower and gazing out over the impressive stretch between the Capitol and the Washington Monument, I wrote my—let me see, now—fourteenth novel, *Paperscape*. It is my first work to have a title conceived in English rather than Russian: I needed something for the Kennan Institute fellowship application.

Paperscape tells the story of a poor soul lost in today's new "scape," the paper world of bureaucracy, politics, journalism, and literature. The novel's hero, an automotive engineer by the name of Igor Velocipedov, is floundering in a flood of certificates, applications, newspaper articles, samizdat manuscripts, denunciations, questionnaires, and dossiers. As a student of yoga (yoga is extremely popular among the rank and file of the Soviet intelligentsia), he wonders whether in addition to the three bodies granted to him by the Heavens (the physical, the astral, and the spiritual) modern man is not granted a fourth, paper, body by the state.

Velocipedov is a rebel. He tried to break with what he perceives as the false, paper, world, but his revolt does no more than help the institutions-that-be to refine their paper image of him. In the end, the hero's literary—that is, paper—escapades land him in emigration (where the Manhattan skyline reminds him of piles of samizdat typescripts).

The irony of it all is that as I worked on the book I came to realize that Americans produce a mighty stream of paper themselves; comparatively speaking, the Soviets produce no more than a trickle. In the USSR the state has a monopoly on bureaucracy; in the USA there is a whole range of bureaucracies, each of them flooding the populace with paper at an alarming rate.

The Soviet state bureaucracy inherited a stodgy, lackluster system from its tsarist predecessor and has succeeded only in entrenching itself deeper and deeper in it. But clumsy and ill equipped as it is, on it creaks, taking forever to prepare the most insignificant document and frustrating both the general public and its own employees in the process.

American bureaucracies are younger and more aggressive than their Russian counterparts; they are energetic, computerized, and exceedingly self-satisfied. The experience of being "processed" by the Immigration and Naturalization Service—and by the Voice of America, when I signed on as a free-lance commentator—has led me to believe that the system actually *enjoys* generating forms. How often have I sweated in front of terrifyingly long sheets of paper with endless paragraphs, dots, and boxes, large print and fine, when all that is wanted is a simple yes or no.

Fortunately, the government does not control all aspects of social life; unfortunately, the government is only one of many structures inundating the paperscape. I say "fortunately" and "unfortunately" though unlike Igor Velocipedov, who gallantly tilts at paper throughout my novel, I see no alternative to the situation as it now stands.

Be that as it may, the more a part of American life I became the more paper I received. Not yet aware of the junk mail phenomenon, I despaired of making my way through the stack of envelopes and packages that piled up on my desk by the end of each week. In an attempt to express my gratitude for the lavish attention paid me by my new hosts, I signed up for eight credit cards (four of which were totally useless), entered into negotiations with three life insurance companies, got caught up in an idiotic sweepstakes, and, fool that I was, nearly rubbed a fork clean of its silver with free sample polish. I joined the AAA twice; I became a member of the Coalition for Clean Air and the Society for the Preservation of the Animal World; I started making regular contributions to the Salvation Army, World Vision, the Spring Daffodil League, and the United Way; I subscribed to six newsweeklies, several of which—*Time,* for one—began coming in two copies; I ordered a $180 jacket (which I could have bought for $140 around the corner) and a lighter in the shape of a World War I cartridge, after which I couldn't possibly help enrolling in the Book-of-the-Month Club and receiving a six-volume biography of a certain Adlai Cooperstein, though fortunately I didn't pay for it because it turned out to have been sent to me by mistake . . .

Then there is the symbiosis between business bureaucrat and computer. Let's say you discover an $800 error in your monthly credit card bill. Needless to say, it is not in your favor. On the one hand, you may derive some satisfaction from the thought that no particular individual is out to get you, that somewhere a computer was simply on its way down; on the other hand, you can't help wondering why the damn thing never errs in your favor, why it always penalizes you and never itself.

It is also a strange feeling to find yourself at the other end of an electronic manhunt. Two and a half years after leaving California I received a bill from Sacramento demanding $1900 in back taxes. The cover letter pointed out—rather optimistically, I imagine—that all attempts by individuals to avoid payment of California taxes have ended in disaster, in other words, the clink.

(I must say that during my stay in California, that is, at the very beginning of my life in America, I hadn't a clue about the American tax system. I was even so naïve as to inquire why the paychecks sent to me by the university amounted to only half the sum the university had agreed to pay me.)

Within the next three days I received as many threatening letters from Sacramento. Clearly the computer had me where it wanted me. Pay up or lockup. I could feel the bars striping my face. Wouldn't the KGB rejoice!

I went to see my accountant. "You've got to save me, Charles!" I told him.

Charles Adams cast a practiced eye over the documents, smiled, and said, "I'll do my best."

A week later the manhunt came to a most unexpected end: the State of California sent me a check for $680. Not only did I not owe a penny; I had a refund coming to me. And you know, it never occurred to me to threaten *the state* with the cooler.

Everything to do with finances is a matter of utter confusion to the newly arrived Soviet émigré. The financial structure of the Soviet Union, at least insofar as it pertains to the ordinary citizen, is at what might be called a piggy bank level: checking accounts do not exist and no one has even heard of credit cards. The only thing a Soviet citizen knows about banks is that they are run by bankers, cigar-toting imperialists all. In short, money matters on a personal level have not changed much since the days of the Golden Horde.

Even after several years in America I am puzzled by this most American of institutions, and although in time we new converts to capitalism learn to deal with such concepts as "negative balance" and "cash flow," I don't ever expect to grasp what goes on with all the various "commodities," what makes bank rates go up and down, and what a deficit balance of payments actually involves. Yet for all my financial ignorance I too have turned into a small-scale financier.

Life in America grants man a fifth body to accompany his fourth or paper body. A financial body. Funds deposited and funds withdrawn are not merely savings and expenses; they are the contours of your financial reality. By depositing and withdrawing, paying bills, and requesting credit, you form a picture of yourself, your image. For not only does the bank draw you into its mysterious ways, it shares its opinion of you with other banks and credit institutions and the Lord knows what else. At first it all seems perfectly absurd and you can't figure out what all these wheeler-dealers (or to translate literally from the Soviet "aces and twisters") want from you, why they are so interested in your piddling savings. Then one day you realize that you've become a small but integral part of their strange way of life and that the bank merely pays the same automatic attention to you as it does to a million or so others.

The form which that attention takes can be a bit shocking to the newcomer. I remember standing open-mouthed on Main Street in Ann Arbor while a hippified young man walked up to a wall, pushed a few buttons, and lo! from the wall there came a great bank note, whereupon the hippie type stuck it in his pocket and walked away content. Now I manipulate automatic tellers with a dexterity that even he might envy, though I must say I've given up on a plan called Chextra that my bank inveigled me into. On one level I know it is meant to enhance my financial well-being; on another I can't get over the feeling it is a form of masked robbery.

I feel even less at home with the relations between tax deductions, mortgages, and interest rates, and have no hope of grasping why it should be more advantageous for me to buy a house and pay the bank enormous interest payments than to lease an apartment and pay the landlord enormous rent—or vice versa. There are times when Maya and I decide we have become Americanized enough to understand it all, but when we sit down to try to work it through we come apart at the seams. Then there are times when we decide nobody understands it all, not even the people who advise us.

And when it comes to investments, we simply pass. Shortly after we left the Soviet Union, my lawyer, Leonard Schroeder, presented us with a tidy little sum he had collected from various publishers. We spent it on a trip to

Europe and the South Pacific. A friend recently told us we could have doubled the money by now with simple investments.

At first the American way of taxes seemed so complex as to be idiotic. How can the system work, we wondered, when accounting firms advertise on TV their skills in finding tax shelters? Only now am I beginning to realize how it influences the way people spend, save, give to charity, open and close businesses, in other words, how it stimulates initiative and ensures regular shots in the arm to the national economy. Only now am I beginning to realize that we were the idiots, not the tax system.

When I look around me and think that almost everyone I see is in one way or another a financier, I really have to hand it to America. Take two men jogging along the river or sitting in a coffee shop or lying by a pool catching some rays. What do you think they're talking about? Well, probably not Plato's *Dialogues* or the poems of Emily Dickinson; probably women or sports or politics. Walk up behind them and what do you hear but a nonchalant, country-club version of the latest in real estate, stock market reports, tax strategies, and the GNP. In fact, even the men who do talk about Plato, even the men who have nothing but irony for the system are deeply involved in its financial metabolism.

Among the most striking differences between Soviet and American society is the difference in the way people spend money. There a lavish purchase or, say, a night out on the town always seems somehow indecent; here spending money is a much respected and socially useful activity. Among the even more striking differences is the difference in the way people learn about what goes on in the economy. The citizen of a society with a "planned economy" has no way of assessing his country's coffers (*Pravda*'s daily hip-hip-hoorays to economic growth and prosperity notwithstanding); the citizen of a free market society has a never-ending stream of hard figures to go by. The Soviet feels he is astride a gigantic inert mass; the American enjoys the sensation of rising and falling; of pulsating activity; it may look chaotic but it is very much alive.

BENEFICENT INEQUALITY

As soon as I began to feel a part of American society, I had to face up to the issue of inequality. In a country where every 250th person you meet in the street is a millionaire (America has a million—that's right, a million—millionaires), the other 249 necessarily suffer from some form of inequality.

The Soviet Union, on the other hand, is the most egalitarian country in the world—as long as you keep in mind what Snowball, the ideologue in *Animal Farm,* said: "All animals are equal, but some animals are more equal than others."

True, even the Soviet Union has its skeptics (sometimes, depending on the political situation, called progressives) who admit that the ideal, the society of "from each according to his abilities, to each according to his needs" is still a thing of the future. "You can't give people what they think they need," say those skeptics. "You'd wind up with gluttony, waste, debauchery, dissipation. No economy could hold out, not even the one that is currently plaguing mankind with its successes."

"The skeptics are wrong, of course," say the idealists (or true believers). "They've been hoodwinked by the capitalists: when they speak of needs, what they have in mind is *capitalist* needs. No, the 'to each according to his needs' ideal is clearly attainable. All it wants is a bit of work on the 'needs' side of things: pare them down to the essentials or teach the population to control them so they vary with variations in the economy, and you've got *Communist* needs!"

Actually, "Communist needs" have been in the making for many years now, and although the process has had its setbacks, it has scored notable success in the field of spiritual (religious, social, cultural) needs, which have been cut back to a stunning near minimum. Moreover, the end is not in sight.

Until 1917 the need for religion in Russia was enormous. It was rooted out overnight. Recently that need has made itself felt again, but the experience amassed in rooting it out the first time can easily return it to its former, minimal, "old woman" status whenever necessary. The need for social and political commitment has currently been satisfied by a single, official, multimillion-member peace organization headed by Yury Zhukov. And the expulsion of a good hundred Russian writers illustrates the present level of the need for literature. History thus demonstrates how the spiritual needs of a nation can be manipulated. (As for history itself, another spiritual need, it has withered away to practically nothing.) In the realm of the spiritual, at least, Soviet society is fast approaching complete and utter equality.

Unfortunately, the same cannot be said of the realm of consumption. Here the Soviet citizen is still grasping, capitalistic; he still wants better-tasting and higher-quality food, better-looking and longer-lasting clothing. But an economy that aspires to equality will never be able to supply these needs: they are needs for *in*equality.

How do we overcome this paradox? Can it be overcome? Yes, but only by strong disciplinary measures that force consumer needs down to a level the economy can supply. The devil of inequality precludes a rise in the quality of life; the god of equality requires a drop in the quality of life. Remember Churchill's famous formula: "The inherent vice of capitalism is the unequal sharing of blessings; the inherent virtue of socialism is the equal sharing of miseries."

For all its brilliance, the aphorism needs a bit of updating. Recent experience with socialism—or what has come to be called real socialism—confirms that it brings about general misery, but likewise shows that it doles out the misery unequally: some have more, some (especially those comrades who are more equal than others) less. Emended, Churchill's words might run as follows: "The inherent vice of capitalism is the unequal sharing of blessings; the inherent virtue of socialism is the unequal sharing of miseries." But even the unhappy prospect of miseries shared unequally suits human nature better than the utopias of equality: utopias, however brilliant their configurations, are horrifying.

What about the poor and destitute, the underclass, as it is now called? How can the proponents of inequality tout our society as an ideal at a time when the media shower us with reports of the homeless and jobless, shelters and soup kitchens? What kind of ideal is that?

No one firmly entrenched in the real world looks ahead to an ideal world. True, the existence of misery and poverty is one of the major social problems of our day, but you don't get rid of poverty by taking "extra" money from the rich and distributing it among the poor. It simply won't last. A dynamic society stands up for its poor with a much more varied and complex program.

The poverty line must allow for a basic level of human dignity. For example, every person should have a place to live, food to eat, clothes to wear. Economic inequality in a framework of human dignity—that's what we should be talking about; a policy *for* the poor rather than *against* the rich—that's economic justice in today's terms.

If there was such a thing as an American Millionaires' Club, it would represent the heart and soul of the country. Social demagoguery has no place in a society where everyone wants to be a millionaire, where inequality encourages people to pull themselves up by their own boot straps and earn more, spend more. The consumer society offers a new kind of equality, an equality based on the marketplace rather than on Marxism or other social theories. A rich man buys a Rolls-Royce for $100,000, a poor man buys a Honda for $5,000. The inequality, the social injustice of it all! But wait. Is the Civic so inferior to the Silver Shadow? It will light your cigarettes and play your tapes; it has a heater and an air-conditioner, first-rate shock absorbers, and comfortable seats. And even if those seats are plastic instead of morocco, it will take you wherever you want to go. As far as actual transportation is concerned, therefore, the rich man and the poor man are all but equal. Though not quite. Many parking garages refuse to take Rollses: the insurance rates are too high. There you have it: discrimination against the rich.

A new style comes into fashion and six-foot models prance about in exorbitant rags. Within weeks a vast industry is churning out imitations at affordable prices. The rich man/poor man shift is all but seamless. Why make the rich poorer when you can make the poor richer?

I'm glad America can support a caste of the dirty rich. How did Fitzgerald put it? "The very rich are different from you and me." The presence of an inaccessible elite makes life more interesting or, let's face it, more fun. I don't need a gold Rolex or a jeweled Concorde, but somehow I get a kick out of knowing that someone somewhere has the ridiculously expensive real thing.

The British make a similar point by supporting queen and crown, and not even the most vehement of Labor governments would dare come out against them. What more wonderful inequality can there be? Prince Charles, in an interview with the American journalist Peter Osnos, displayed an acute awareness of his role as the absolute standard of Britishness. Osnos, who happens to look and dress remarkably like the prince, pointed out to me later—not without a certain satisfaction—that the prince's suit had cost at least twice as much as his.

Today's poor enjoy luxuries only recently limited to the rich. For a fiver they can hire the services of the world's finest orchestras; for a tenner they can own a first-class museum collection. The video revolution offers untold possibilities, transatlantic flights keep coming down in price, home computers are spreading like wildfire . . . With this strange new world comes a strange new equality amid inequality, and if Marxists argue it isn't genuine equality, then I say, Thank goodness!

Of *political* equality and inequality in America I lack personal experience, having no rights at all except the right to return from trips abroad. Once I have dutifully paid my taxes for five years, I will receive American citizenship and the right to participate in the great battle of the elephant and the donkey. For the time being I can't say I have any strong feelings about the American political structure except for one: that it should remain as is.

It doesn't ever seem to occur to Americans that their democracy could fall or even falter. To those of us who come here from Eastern Europe, however, American democracy at first seems as fragile, as vulnerable as Little Red Riding Hood in the forest. Accustomed as we are to the brute lawlessness of our former governments, we tend to look upon democracy as weak. We fear for it.

Take Watergate, for instance, when the American press took advantage of its right to criticize any individual, including the president, and the *Washington Post* all but ran him out of office. Many Russian émigrés maintain that the crisis in the American presidency led to the establishment of totalitarian regimes in several countries of Asia and Africa, the annihilation of three million Cambodians, and a global drop in the prestige of the democratic system. They are afraid of what will happen if history repeats itself. Will it be the "last and decisive battle" prophesied by the Soviet Communist party anthem? Will the United States come tumbling down?

It is hard for former Soviets to see the other point of view; it is hard for us to see Watergate as one of the cataclysms essential to the *consolidation* of American democracy. And it is hard for us to understand that as patriotic as the great majority of Americans are, they do not identify their

country with its government. The Communists constantly
drummed into our heads that the party *is* the Soviet
Union—the country, the state, the epitome of national
pride and patriotism. They even delved into metaphysics to
instill in us the most bizarre of postulates, namely: "The
people and the party are one!"

America's size and power automatically lead Soviets to
assume that America and the Soviet Union are the same in
certain respects, that, for instance, there is a single (perhaps invisible) center controlling the entire country. How
else could so vast an area be held in check or set in motion?

A few winters ago some of my students at Johns Hopkins
and Goucher went to the Soviet Union as tourists. They
came back full of excitement, yet disturbed by some of the
talks they'd had. "We got the impression that many of the
people we talked to think the States is a totalitarian country.
Seriously. They wanted to know all about the brainwashing
we have to go through. They're certain that the FBI is
everywhere, that, like, colleges and universities are swarming with informers, criticism of the administration is nipped
in the bud, telephones are bugged, letters opened and cen-
sored—and that the whole shebang is masterminded by
that evil dictator Ronald Reagan. We didn't know what to
do. Nothing we could say seemed to make a dent in them.
And did we feel weird defending ourselves against that kind
of accusation in the Soviet Union!"

The simplest response would have been to quote them
their own Russian proverb: "Other cows may moo, not
yours" (which corresponds more or less to the pot calling
the kettle black), but I think the students were right to push
on with their explanations. The thing is that not only the
people who seemed so misguided to them—that is, not
only people who are bombarded by daily, hourly anti-
American propaganda and therefore spew it back—but independent thinkers too have their doubts about the United
States. "Europe—now that's where you've got true democ-

racy. America—well, how shall I put it, everything is decided at the top and the leaders are tough and you've got the military industrial complex and the FBI and the CIA and all that." Few people have a true idea of how democratic American society is and how widespread criticism or, rather, pluralism is.

The Soviet press often brands President Reagan a "second Hitler" (passing over Stalin in silence). No Soviet intellectuals believe it, of course, but even they have no concept of America's unceremonious approach to its president. True, Russians love to tell jokes about their leaders and Americans don't, as a rule, go around telling Reagan jokes, but the reason is not, as *Literaturnaya gazeta* might speculate, that Americans fear the FBI; the reason is that as soon as Reagan jokes crop up they are turned into cartoons and reproduced millions of times in newspapers and magazines, that is, in what Soviet propaganda calls the American propaganda machine.

I very much enjoyed the recent spat over the 1600 block on Pennsylvania Avenue. When the evening news announced that for security reasons the White House intended to close that stretch of Pennsylvania Avenue to traffic, the local press overflowed with protests. "Penn belongs to the people of Washington," the mayor declared, "not to President Reagan." I'd like to see the Moscow Town Council stand up to Gorbachev like that!

Walking past one of Washington's array of left-leaning bookshops recently (it was a ten-minute walk from the White House, by the way), I noticed a poster called "The Anatomy of Our President" in the window. There stood Ronald Reagan stripped to his shorts, arrows leading from various parts of his anatomy to brief texts. *The President's Ears:* the left one doesn't work; he hears messages only from the right. *The President's Arms:* overdeveloped. *The President's Heart:* in top shape—he sleeps eighteen hours a day. Needless to say, the lower the arrows the lower the humor.

That's America. But since Reagan is an American, the digs don't particularly bother him. All in all, I must say I admire the man. He has a good sense of humor and even a certain self-irony, healthy qualities in a statesman. And when that bullet hit him in the chest, his face showed not a shadow of fear. The whole country has seen it a hundred times: the bullet strikes home and he glares into the crowd, searching out his attacker. The leader of another large country is known to have shat himself in circumstances a good deal less drastic.

After five years in America I can't help laughing when I read about the "American propaganda machine" that Reagan supposedly manipulates with such skill. I know from my own experience how hard it is for the Soviet reader to grasp that the American mass media have nothing to do with the government, that (with the exception of the official United States Information Agency, of course) they serve as a kind of opposition.

At times the newsmen almost seem to gang up on the president, going into the details of his latest checkup, counting up all his lymphocytes, poking about in his gut with the surgeons. In the Soviet Union a leader's intestines are a carefully guarded state secret. As for the TV commentators, they seem to consider it their duty to pick at his every word. Doubt first, check later—that's their motto. The moment the president says there is a need for more discipline in the schools, images of orderly classrooms flash on the screen. If he had said there was too much discipline, they'd have shown a blackboard jungle.

The intellectual who proffers even a few kind words for the president faces ostracism: he no longer fits the left-leaning, antiauthoritarian, liberal stereotype that intellectual circles have spawned. At first, Russian émigrés were horrified by the intellectuals' position, but they have gradually come to see that the coexistence of a number of views is what makes America strong, that its strength depends to a large extent on its flexibility, the interchangeability of its parts.

MY FIRST PRESIDENTIAL CAMPAIGN

Some of the psychological structures American democracy is based on are still unclear to me. We Soviet Americanophiles had always thought that the democratic process required a special brand of irreproachable people, but no—it muddles along with perfectly ordinary ones, some of whom are simpletons or show-offs or self-seekers but most of whom combine the most various ingredients. Sorting out the ingredients and making an intelligent choice every few years—in other words, electing officials—seems an onerous burden to people who have spent their lives in an atmosphere of totalitarian fraud. One giant, all-encompassing fraud is simpler than a multitude of petty tricks and deceptions.

In the movie *Moscow on the Hudson* a recent Russian arrival swoons in a supermarket, unable to choose a brand of coffee from among the dozens lining the shelves. Too great a choice places too great a strain on his unpracticed faculties.

I myself experienced the same sort of vertigo watching the nine Democratic presidential candidates debate on television. Perhaps the selection was a bit too generous. In any case, thanks to America's wise and farsighted immigration laws, I had no vote. I could have sat back and taken it easy, but I couldn't help wondering which candidate I would have voted for. They all sounded so high-minded. How was I to determine whose was the highest mind of all?

In the end I decided to work through my doubts in an imaginary representative of today's Moscow intelligentsia, an internal émigré of sorts, a combination Childe Harold and Sancho Panza. Let us call him Phil Phophanophph.

Imagine, if you will, that to avoid censorship we correspond by means of carrier pigeon.

Washington

Dear Phil,

This is the first time I've been able to observe an American electoral campaign from soup to nuts. Every evening our living room comes alive with the echoes of "primaries" and "caucuses" (no relation to our Caucasus) and similar mysterious events.

Remember when we decided to stop voting? Back in '56, wasn't it? Those ballots! "Choose one candidate. Cross out the others." And you said, "But look, there *are* no 'others.' Do they think we're imbeciles or something?" From then on, our Pavlovian reaction to elections was nausea.

Now I feel drawn to the process. Nor am I alone in the émigré community. Once the usual Andropov or Chernenko jokes are out of the way, we start in on the latest caucuses, move on to the question of charisma, and end up shouting, with the rest of the nation, "Where's the beef?"

What's going on? I wonder. Is it some unconscious human need or just the excitement of a football fan?

Moscow

Dear Vassily,

Surprise! This year your American elections happen to coincide with our Soviet elections! Just as I was reading your letter, I heard a knock at the door. A pretty girl came in and said, "Greetings, Comrade! I'm your local Agitprop canvasser. I'm here to register your name, age, and sex for the coming Supreme Soviet elections."

"You've come just in time," I said. "Could you fill me in

on the differences between Soviet elections and American elections?"

She looked it up in her *Agitprop Canvasser's Guide.* "In American elections all candidates are protégés of the military industrial complex."

"What you mean is American voters have no choice, is that it?"

The pretty little Agitprop canvasser shrugged her shoulders and sighed. "Why ask provocative questions, Comrade?" she said. "Just tell me what to write in the 'sex' column. Male? . . ."

Washington

Dear Phil,

The day before yesterday one of those "protégés" of the military industrial complex made a frontal attack on the B-1 bomber project. In a speech to a university audience he pledged to cut some choice bits from the war machine and pass them on to poor starving students. Clearly he expected a burst of applause of the kind once accorded the man they now compare him to, but for some reason the students remained silent.

Fortunately, none of this has anything to do with me: I haven't been here long enough to judge the candidates by their philosophies or intellectual prowess. The only thing I can judge is their looks.

As far as I can tell, they're all quite attractive: tall, slim, well-tailored suits, neat hair, no bald spots in attendance. (Apparently a bald man would stand little chance of being elected.) Of course the candidates are not the best-looking people the country has to offer, but they're not supposed to be the *best* of anything. If they were, they'd have to be the best of everything.

The one thing they need besides charm (or "charisma" as they call it here) is a record. Each one claims to have a better record than the others. I can't say I know quite what they have in mind, so I'm still concentrating on their looks.

Moscow

Dear Vassily,

Your "physical" approach to the American hopefuls has given me new insight into our own problems. It may even hold the key to a way out of our mono-party self-elections. With this in mind I decided to request an appointment with the all-powerful Comrade N, secretary of the Writers Union and a delegate to the Supreme Soviet.

"Why not have two candidates for the same office, Comrade N? They can both be members of our Sole and Solely Possible Party, but one of them will have curly hair and the other will, say, walk with a limp. That will give people a choice and shut up those bourgeois slandermongers who keep calling our elections a sham."

"It won't work," Comrade N grunted after a long silence. "The people will never be able to decide for themselves whether curly hair is better than a club foot. Besides, a candidate's physical aspect may temporarily blind them to the indisputable perfection of Marxist theory. Our party has decided once and for all that one is better than two. I hope you find my explanation satisfactory, Citizen Phophanophph. And may I advise you NOT TO STICK YOUR GODDAMN NECK OUT AGAIN! That will be all."

Washington

Dear Phil,

Since I last wrote, a few graybeards have dropped by the wayside, but the campaign itself is going strong. The fewer the candidates, the greater the number of variables in the candidates still in the running: their wrinkles, their age (as opposed to how old they say they are), their skin coloration, their ability to keep their mouths shut, their proximity to certain prototypes or distance from all prototypes, the hair on their faces and the way they part the hair on their heads . . . Oh yes, and their supply of "new ideas."

I'm gradually coming to realize there is no ideal combination, but how to choose the *best* combination? I don't think I've got the knack of democracy yet. Isn't there something arrogant and aristocratic about preferring one person to another? I keep wondering how to resolve this and other contradictions.

MOSCOW

Dear Vassily,

Follow Pushkin's advice: Uncork a bottle of champagne and reread *The Marriage of Figaro.*

Sketches *for a Novel to Be*

1 9 8 5 / Bursting into the novel like the flying spirit of America zooms Mr. Flitflint, one of those types who wear T-shirts until mid-January and wave an enormous cardboard finger over their heads at the Super Bowl. He'll pull his Cherokee Chief into the Fenimore Cooper Service Area off a fast-flowing Interstate 95 to piss away the excess suds, check his biorhythms, munch a burger, and jerk off the joystick of a videogame. Then, seven and a half minutes later, *z-o-o-o-m!*

1 9 8 3 / The HMN goes to an experimental theater located under the Santa Melinda Freeway, just to the right of the tunnel entrance. During the intermission he sends the following note backstage: "Why not have your Romeo stop on his way to the balcony, wrap himself in the curtain, and balloon like an agave plant, thus evoking the inexorability of his desire? Why not have your Mercutio ride a unicycle, juggling torches as symbols of the Renaissance? I am categorically opposed to the Nurse's appearance stage left! She must parachute down from the rafters . . ." And so on. Sixty-four pointers in all.

Soon the whole town is buzzing about a brilliant new production. When the HMN goes back, he sees Romeo ballooning like an agave plant, Mercutio pedaling away and swallowing fire, the Nurse—her leg in a cast—dangling center stage in a parachute. After the performance the director comes out and points to a man in the audience. "Ladies and gentlemen! I give you the second Stanislavsky-Nemirovich-Danchenko, the third Meyerhold, the fourth Lyubimov, the top banana of Moscow's theater world, Mr.—Hmm-m-m . . ."

So the HMN has been recognized, appreciated! A new chapter in his American odyssey has begun.

1 9 8 5 / Mr. Flitflint, America's flying spirit, suddenly comes down with an attack of spleen. All the beaches of Malibu can't help him. He's jaded.

So on to Europe, and here we are in Europe. Things are really jumping. And at the sight of Flitflint's MasterCard International the locals all jump too. After a strenuous day at the café, on comes the bow tie. Oysters, gigot, crème brûlée—it's all in a night's play. MasterCard International Adventures nonstop.

8 Several years ago, when Western Europe was one large anti-American demonstration, I broached the issue of anti-American sentiment with an Important Personage in Washington. "It's sheer ingratitude," I said. "Twice America helped them out of war, twice America helped them to rebuild and set up a buffer along the eastern borders. Where do the negative feelings come from, and why do they stretch from left to right, across the entire political spectrum?"

"Elementary," said the Important Personage. "We're rich; they're jealous."

"Is a Mercedes jealous of a Cadillac?"

"Touché," he said. "They're not poor anymore. But we're still the richest."

So Americans still cling to a thirty-year-old cliché, a vision of their country as the richest and most powerful, their science the most advanced, their movies the most entertaining, their athletes the strongest, and so on—no proof required. (In fact, it might be all this and more, but proof *is* required.)

Even now I can't get over how Americans call the fall baseball orgy the *World* Series when basically only Americans are involved. The implication is that foreigners, clearly inferior, need not apply. By the same token, the champions of the NFL and NBA are *world* champs. Now both may be tops in what they do (especially the football players, since American-style football does not exist outside the United States), but you don't become a *world* champion unless you compete for *world* supremacy.

American intellectuals tend to interpret this attitude as a spin-off of superpower chauvinism; I see it as a kind of provincial strongman act. "I'm the strongest man in the world!" roars the bruiser, rattling his chains.

Is it this *a priori* feeling of superiority that so isolates America from Europe, or is it America's isolation that keeps the feeling alive? In any case, it grates on America's well-wishers, even us new Americans. In the Soviet Union we pictured Americans as "citizens of the world," cosmopolitans; here we find them to be detached, withdrawn, sequestered in their American planet.

To go back to sports. I always used to rant and rave about how Soviet television gave inadequate coverage to certain international competitions. I naturally put it down to the specifics of Soviet society and its hermetically sealed ideology. Imagine my amazement when I discovered soon after my arrival that to all intents and purposes international sports do not exist for American audiences. Furiously racing through the buttons on my TV set, I could find no newscast coverage, much less actual matches. America's concept of sport as human activity is totally new to me, and I was a long time getting used to it.

At the time we arrived in the States, the Canadian Cup international hockey finals happened to be on. In the USSR the Canadian Cup is a major event: what's at stake is not only whether the Red Army Athletic Club will overpower the "haughty superstars" of professional hockey but—subliminally, at least—whether socialism will win out over capitalism. The moment the Canadian Cup goes on the air the streets are empty.

American television passed over the great event in silence. All I could find on the screen was a bunch of droopy-assed, beer-bellied candidates for middle age waving cudgels at a ball, then trying to circle a diamond in their long johns, and occasionally throwing sand at a man with a cage over his face. Afraid of sinking into ignorance, I checked all the newspapers. At last, deep in the sports pages of the *New York Times* I spied a tiny filler: the Russians had trounced the NHL All Stars 8 to 2. I doubt that anyone but a handful of Russian émigrés bothered to track down the information.

When the time for the Stanley Cup finals rolled around, there was a spate of news items and locker-room interviews: the "real" event—that is, the American event—had begun. One evening at about that time I saw a feature—on NBC, I think—that made me gasp. It was called "Can Ivan Play Hockey?" and told the story of Victor Nechaev, a Leningrad hockey player who had married an American, moved to the States, and signed with the Los Angeles Kings. "Will you look at that!" the commentator marveled. "This Ivan really knows how to play our game!" In his ignorance the man had never heard that the "Ivans" had for many years been hockey champions of the world, creaming the best the NHL had to offer. "Look at him go, folks! Can he skate! Can he use that stick! Where did he learn his tricks, I wonder?"

Actually, Victor (I have since made his acquaintance) had played several seasons of top league Soviet hockey. Ask him what he thinks about the California Kings and he shrugs. "Child's play." A typically laconic response.

If an American or, say, a Laplander joined a Russian team, the Russians would go crazy over him. In a closed society like the Soviet Union, public interest (and not only in sports) is directed outward, while in open, democratic America it is almost wholly inner directed. The outside world interests Americans much less, either because they assume, *a priori,* that it is worse than their American world or because that American world is simply too overpowering.

The press roundly criticized ABC for its coverage of the 1984 Olympics, calling it chauvinistic, Americocentric. I agree. During all those weeks (and I followed events very closely) I waited in vain for an interpreter-assisted interview. How interesting, how *entertaining* to talk to a Chinese, a Hindu, a Frenchman, a Lesothian! But no, the people at ABC could find no one note- or newsworthy among the 140 delegations until the final day, when a dark horse Portuguese won the men's marathon.

Yet is ABC really to blame? On the one hand, their self-justification sounds fully justified: the audience simply didn't care; on the other hand—and here the situation closely parallels the situation in all the media—an audience develops under the influence of what the medium supplies. It's a classic vicious circle.

Despite the iron curtain the Soviet Union is in many ways closer to Europe than Europe's closest political and economic partner, America. Or, to put it in more concrete terms, Soviet goalies have an easier time crossing the iron curtain than American quarterbacks crossing the Atlantic.

FOOTBALL MINUS FEET

It's uncanny how quickly the "ours/theirs" distinction develops here. You'd think a country populated by countless nationalities would produce a hothouse of cosmopolitanism; what happens instead is that the exiles, refugees, and displaced persons turn into Americans long before they qualify for citizenship.

I too keep catching myself reacting spontaneously in ways I know to be American. Yet at first all kinds of things irritated me. The smell of popcorn in movie theaters, for instance. Smells in general—all those peanut butters, catsups, and tacos. It may be partly a question of biochemistry. In fact, homesickness may be more biochemical than psychological. Remember, we haven't merely crossed a border; we've crossed an ocean. America is a different planet in a sense. The chemistry of the water, air, soil, and foliage is different (infinitesimally, perhaps, but different), so the bread, milk, fruits, and vegetables are different too.

If some smells are more pungent, however, others have

faded. Émigrés are often maddened by the general lack of smells. "Strawberries don't smell," "People don't sweat"—such are the clichés of émigré conversation. And clichés are not necessarily wrong. Last summer in Paris we walked into a meeting and recoiled from the acrid smell of perfume mixed with sweat. "Hmm," we said, exchanging glances. "Back home people don't perspire like that."

Football naturally made me hopping mad. Europe is throbbing with major battles; hundreds of thousands of fans pour endless psychic energy into the most minute movements of their favorites—and here they don't even call it football. No, here it's soccer, a name whose similarity to "socks" gives the sport a kind of sissified reputation, while the exciting word "football" is reserved for a game in which foot hits ball only three or four times in the course of an hour. Strange: the ball travels from hand to hand, but the game isn't called handball; the ball (though I'd rather not dignify that pigskin by the name of ball) travels under the arm, but the game isn't called armball. "Football" is a complete misnomer.

On many an evening in dreary Ann Arbor digs, in motel rooms across the country, in a Santa Monica flat that differed from a motel room only in that we had to change our own sheets, I watched the bumblings of brawn in padded shoulders and virtually bulletproof helmets—what Soviet propaganda decries as the apotheosis of the American cult of violence and cruelty, an imperialist form of sport in which all the players do is knock out their opponents' teeth and pick up their own—and thought, "How dull!"

I had even experienced it live. One day a couple of professors from the University of Michigan Slavic Department took me to a home game and I learned how a touchdown was scored, why the crowds cheered, and when the bands marched. Just in front of us sat a middle-aged couple in feather-trimmed cowboy hats, billing and cooing as if there were no game in progress. Then, at half time, over the stadium flew a Cessna trailing a banner with the message MARGIE, MARRY ME! LOVE, DOUG. The couple jumped up, glowing beyond what would have seemed the limits of the human skin. "That's me! I'm Doug! She's Margie! It doesn't cost that much! Two hundred bucks! Your very own feelings plastered across the sky! And she's said yes!"

In the end, Doug's "heavenly" declaration of love was as much the high point of the game for me as it was for the lovebirds. The vicissitudes of the "football" left me cold, and for a long time I went on stalking the sports pages of the émigré press for the real thing. I never dreamed I would soon succumb to Redskin fever.

It all began in 1983, when the Redskins beat the Dolphins and copped the championship. My wife and I drove into Georgetown to see how the fans would celebrate. We were hardly prepared for what we saw: crowds dancing in the streets, in windows, on the roofs of buildings and cars; fireworks everywhere. All hail the Redskins! All hail the world champs!

After that triumph for our city (oh, that American community spirit!) I started getting more into football. I learned why an effective defensive front needed experienced linebackers and defensive backs; I learned about reverse T formations and scramble blocking. I discovered to my amazement that compared with hockey, football is almost polite. When I tried to explain all this to a visiting Soviet, once a major athlete himself, he stood up from the TV set and announced solemnly, "A country that plays this game is invincible!"

"But this is the only country where it's played," I replied.

Our guest looked at me in astonishment. "I didn't mean *football,*" he said.

"Then what did you mean?"

"Don't you see?" he said. "Invincible in everything."

My guest's reaction was typical of the global approach to sport common in the Soviet Union.

. . .

On the snowy evening of January 22, 1984, we had something more specific in mind: the Skins were slated to meet the Raiders at the Super Bowl. Would they repeat their triumph? On our way to the bowl we had trounced our big rivals, the Cowboys, beat the mighty Forty-niners to a pulp, and destroyed the Rams. "You can't play them," a Ram stated publicly. "They're too damn good." Washington bars rocked to the strains of "Washington Redskins, World's Finest Football Machine" (a takeoff on the "Rasputin" song?).

The teams arrived in Tampa a week early: the fans followed in jam-packed jets. Everything was set for a carnival. "Sorry, pals," Joe Theismann, John Riggins, and Dave Watts clowned for the cameras, "but you're in for it." And then . . . Hard as it is to bring it all back, the Redskins suffered a humiliating defeat. Nothing went right for them that day. The Raiders' quarterback made passes that led President Reagan to compare him to a secret weapon and fear that the Soviets would call for his dismantling.

That night a neighbor asked me hopefully, "You don't understand the game, do you?" "All too well," I replied.

I really had begun to understand—and not only football. After a few years here you find yourself changing. My cosmopolitan enthusiasm is waning. Willy-nilly I am being sucked into the great big colorful world of American provincialism.

Sketches for a Novel to Be

1985/ It is the height of summer. The humidity is 100 percent. Our hero gets into a taxi with an American girl. She is a physically fit specimen of forty or so with a luxuriant mane of hair and treasure chest of teeth—a TV network princess or a baroness of the military industrial complex.

"Let me loosen your tie! Ha-ha-ha. Don't believe those rumors you've heard about how wild I am. I just like to undo men's ties."

They had just met. There had been a theft in the house. A bottle. "I've remained true to the principle of alcoholic kleptomania since the construction of Akademgorodok in Novosibirsk. Care for a slug?"

"Are you always so casual with celebrities?"

"Only in emigration."

Their driver that night was Louis Armstrong. He peered in the rearview mirror at the two laughing mouths—one first class, the other of dubious quality. Where were they from?

"From a Russian party. Have you ever been to one, Satchmo?"

Mr. Armstrong sighed with all his alveoli and said, "I've got a Russian party in my soul."

FROM A COLLECTION OF EPIGRAPHS

"The North American States attract the attention of the most thoughtful of people. . . . America is calmly carrying out its mission, secure and flourishing, . . . proud of its institutions. But certain deep minds . . . have undertaken investigations there, and their reports have rekindled issues long presumed resolved."

—Alexander Pushkin

"America represents the image of democracy as such, with all its flaws and merits, prejudices and passions. . . . It is an issue involving not only the United States but also the whole world."

—Alexís de Tocqueville

"The USA is the principal representative of modern capitalism. . . . Its economy is subject to cyclical crises. . . . After World War II imperialist circles in the USA unleashed the 'cold war' against the USSR and other Socialist states. . . . Given shifting relations of power in the world and thanks primarily to the increase in power of the USSR, the USA has been forced to take a series of steps in the direction of normalization."

—The Soviet Encyclopedic Dictionary

"The USA may turn out to be the last bastion of capitalism."

—Vladimir Mayakovsky

"We praised everything [in America]. . . . Once we were riding along and a man put his hand in my pocket, took out my brush, and started brushing his hair. All we did was exchange glances."

—Fyodor Dostoyevsky, *The Possessed*

1 9 8 5 / According to *Entertainment Tonight,* Jane Fonda has confessed to *Star* magazine that for the past twenty (20!) years she has suffered from compulsive gluttony and that to keep the pride and joy of all progressive mankind

in shape she has had to stick her finger down her throat several times a day.

Jane! For the HMN, who happened to be going through a fit of deep existentialism at the time, your confession had the force of an explosion of mustard gas. You mean even way back when—though it was well within the twenty-year period—even way back when, darling, you were heaving and ho-ing and tossing your cookies several times a day?

9 One gray muggy morning—the worst Washington has to offer—I was wending my way to Kalorama Triangle, my goal some soda pop and a pack of cigarettes, when suddenly, at the end of Columbia Road, I spied a parade. What was the occasion? Where were the laboring masses headed? The closer they came, the less they looked like the May Day variety. No, they were a motley bunch complete with floats, festoons, and balloons. In fact, they put me in mind of one of Fellini's marvelous processions. And then I realized what it was: Washington's gay community on the march!

Nothing out of the ordinary, of course: beefy men in pink ruffled dresses and pasty makeup; closely cropped women in jackets and ties. Curiously, in the midst of all the bacchanalia it was not the raging queens or the cowboy stuffed into black leather seatless chaps who looked strange; it was the grim ranks of the "ideologicals," gays who do not stand out in a crowd of straights, who have ordinary male and female faces except that they are overlaid with a "message." A movement that began as a struggle against social hypocrisy has taken on the traits of a mighty ideology and has thereby acquired its own brand of hypocrisy.

Once I appeared on a network television talk show that went on the air with the roosters. "Who's going to watch at this hour?" I asked my host. "Seven million people whose sleeping pills didn't work," he replied cheerfully.

(Several people with an unhealthy pallor waved to me in the street that morning.)

My job was to answer the insomniacs' queries, most of which accurately reflected the low level of the Western giant's understanding of the Eastern giant. From San Francisco, for example, came the following question: "To what degree does the Soviet gay community express its rights in politics and public life in general?"

"Alas," I had to reply, "not at all. Male homosexuality is considered a criminal offense and is punishable by a prison term of three years."

I had the distinct impression that my West Coast questioner did not believe me.

Imagine what a recent émigré thinks when he first comes across gay pride parades and the gay press. Of course, America has come a long way from its original level of sexual hypocrisy, and hypocrisy here must have been worse than in Russia if even today certain states maintain laws against oral sex. Like other forms of liberalization in America, however, sexual liberalization has gone a bit too far. It has ballooned into an obsession, a craze, a mass orgy; it has bad taste written all over it.

During my first trip to the States I heard a TV preacher berating his fellow citizens for indulging in mass sodomy. "There are twenty million homosexuals in this country," he thundered. "Where are we going?"

"Twenty million?" I remember thinking then. "Impossible." Now I realize it was just another American obsession. The statistics obsession or, rather, the obsession with *terrifying* statistics.

Americans feel that numbers should stun. Where do the mind-boggling figures in Soviet anti-American propaganda come from? In his novel about America, subtly titled *The Face of Hatred,* the Soviet writer Vitaly Karotich cites an American source for the assertion that there are thirty million starving people living in the United States. Wait a second, I say (to myself, not to Karotich). Every seventh person? You mean every seventh person in the country lacks the wherewithal to fill his stomach? With so many people on diets, is anyone eating?

Every morning the newscasters astound us with figures. Eight hundred thousand Americans had partial hearing loss in the left ear last year; six million saw doctors for flat feet. One day I heard that there were two million kidnaped children in America. How many children are there altogether? Fifty, sixty million? If one in every thirty children is gone, disappeared, then why are we sitting at home watching television? Why aren't we out there looking for them? When I looked into it, I found a lengthy FBI report admitting that the number is actually . . . well, rather exaggerated. It's not two million; it's thirty thousand. And half of them are runaways. And two thirds of the rest were taken by a divorced parent. A zero here, a zero there . . . Somebody seems to have been trying too hard.

Now what about the twenty million homosexuals? Taking the figure of twenty million as a base, we can extrapolate twenty-seven million homosexuals in the Soviet Union and close to a hundred million in China. I don't know about China, but in the Soviet Union the "light blue division" (as homosexuals are called there) is far from numerous. If our figure was anywhere near accurate, there would be a gay gulag the likes of which no one can imagine.

I may be wildly wide of the mark, but it is my impression that a large number of America's recent homosexuals are merely part of America's latest obsession. I put it down partly to the innocence of American youth and partly to an aesthetic crisis, the loss of a sense of moderation and taste.

I have nothing against homosexuality. On the contrary, I have always felt sympathetic to the *true* light blue division because of what its members have suffered as victims of pietism and sanctimony. We have a married gay couple living on the floor above us—two musicians, one black, one white; they are an integral part of our Adams Morgan melting pot, and things would be drearier without them. But I draw the line when it comes to forcing a homosexual life-style on others; I am against forcing *any* life-style on others.

MADAME SOVCENS

America's obsession with obsessions is for some reason often connected with the nether regions of the body or, in a word, with sex. American sex life knows no peace, only eternal flailing. Take the feminist movement or, rather, its antimale fringe group. Let me tell you about a curious confrontation I had with them before I learned to recognize the Amazon look.

I was attending a university-sponsored conference on "The Writer and Human Rights," where I was scheduled to participate in a panel on censorship. The word "censorship" in Russian is feminine. As funny as that fact sounds to speakers of English, it remains a fact. In Russian, as in most European languages, people, things, and concepts are divided by gender. "Joy" *(radost)* is female, "ecstasy" *(vostorg)* male. There are also words that float in an amorphous neuter gender, words like "state" *(gosudarstvo)*. What fun for Freudian (feminist, homosexual, structural, deconstructionist) interpretation!

The Czech speaker who preceded me concluded with words to the effect that "she would never succeed in her attempt to suppress the creative spirit of Central Europe." The "she" here referred to censorship: in Czech, as in Russian, the word is feminine. Our hosts, the American writers, may have shuddered slightly at the solecistic "she," but they put up with it. They show great tact in dealing with our attempts to turn our thoughts into the language of Shakespeare.

Now it was my turn to show off an English that one journalist has characterized as "more epigrammatical than grammatical." "If censorship in our Slavic world was a 'she,' " I began, "she was a rather hysterical old hag. Once upon a time she had been young; some had even found her attractive. She had ruined things for herself, however, by demanding an all-consuming, unequivocal love. Poor Madame Sovcens! With age she has grown more and more frustrated: writers keep defaulting in their amorous duties. True, she still rushes about, powdering herself desperately with Socialist realism, but in vain. No one loves her anymore."

As I delved deeper into my dubious metaphor, I noticed an occasional hiss, but by the time I came to a stopping point the hissing had turned to loud boos. A pink-cheeked creature with short bangs jumped up and shouted, "How dare you!" A defiant wave of the arm revealed two mounds beneath a bulky sweater. "How dare you compare Soviet censorship to a woman!"

"Perhaps I haven't made myself clear," I stuttered. "I only . . ."

"Stop, stop, stop," she cried, very much the commissar. "You've made yourself all too clear. You've insulted all people of the female sex present here today."

A very nonacademic hubbub arose. "But ladies and gentlemen!" I cried amid shouts of "Disgraceful" and "Male chauvinist pig." "I mean, women and men! I mean, comrades! It was all a joke! A metaphor! Nothing else!" An analogous scene from *The World According to Garp* had suddenly come to mind, and my flesh was crawling.

Luckily, a sympathetic feminist (of the male variety) came to the rescue. "Can't you see?" he shouted over the din. "It's the centuries of Russian slavery that does it to him!"

"Yes, yes!" I cried. "That must be why we metaphorically refer to the Soviet power structure by a woman's name, Stepanida Vlasyevna, and . . ."

"Then do you apologize?" the pink activist interrupted, suddenly conciliatory.

"Oh, yes! With all my heart. And from this moment on, the metaphor—all metaphors—will cease to exist."

Which is how I got off easily on the censorship panel at the conference on "The Writer and Human Rights."

Looking back at the episode, I am forced to admit to a rather negative attitude to a certain *Soviet* brand of feminism. It dates from the thirties and is symbolized for me by the distinctly masculine features of the famous pilot Marina Grizodubova. Women became superstars of labor, heroines of Socialist competition, and "servants of the people," that is, deputies of the Supreme Soviet. What they never became was *masters* of the people. The only woman to crack the Politburo has been Yekaterina Furtseva, and then only for a short term. (She was soon kicked out and sent over to run culture, apparently because the men considered culture woman's work.)

Nowadays virtually nothing remains of the principles set down by the famous feminist radicals of the twenties like Larisa Reisner and Alexandra Kollontai. There are almost no women in the armed forces, diplomatic corps, or government. There are, however, plenty of women in construction, women who wield picks and shovels while a man so drunk he can barely hold his pencil straight supervises them. By the age of thirty the average woman laborer or peasant has forgotten the art of love; she lacks the time and energy for sex, to say nothing of Amazon tactics.

Women with white-collar jobs, especially women in the major cities, knock themselves out trying to keep up with Western styles. One of the great Moscow mysteries is how secretaries making 120 rubles a month manage to parade around in Italian boots which, if you're lucky, you can find on the black market for 200 rubles. Suddenly lipstick vanishes; suddenly some wild economic hurricane sweeps away all panty hose, bras, perfume, bikinis, nail polish, mascara, face powder—hundred of women's accessories are in a constant state of flux. The Soviet woman is so involved in making herself attractive she has no thoughts of dominating men. Add the search for decent food, which is in that same mysterious state of flux as well, and you get a truly terrifying piece of statistics: Soviet urban woman spends about twenty hours a week in lines.

The official Soviet women's movement, the Committee of Soviet Women, bears little relation to the reality of women's lives; the unofficial women's movement, founded by a group of Leningrad enthusiasts and responsible for a samizdat journal called *Maria,* was soon smothered by an asexual police bent on destroying everything that lacks the approval of the "proper authorities."

Russia is a country long rife with frustrated women ("How about dropping by this evening, Ivan—I'll have a bottle of vodka ready"), and although the bundle of American obsessions known as the sexual revolution might have brought them a bit more pleasure, it has not increased their freedom by one iota. The female half of the erotic act has always been demeaned in Russia. Even lexically. In English you can say, "She fucked him," thereby acknowledging the woman's initiative. The equivalent in Russian sounds strange, almost ungrammatical. Yet Russian has no end of expressions to debase and defile women, slam them down spread-eagled under a mighty stud. So there was in fact something to the "years of slavery" claim made by my savior at the conference.

How do "years of freedom" influence American sexual values, postrevolution style? Once I was invited to speak to a creative writing class at a women's college. When the instructor asked me to assign a story of mine, I suggested "The Destruction of Pompeii," which had recently been published in the *Partisan Review* and which depicts the decadent Roman resort in terms strikingly reminiscent of the Soviet resort town of Yalta.

During the class we spoke about everything except the story. Clearly none of the students had read it. Afterward

I asked the instructor, who seemed the picture of a progressive woman, why she had decided not to pass it out.

"Oh, I couldn't give our girls a story with all that sex." She blushed.

We parted with shrugs and vague glances, whereupon she went off to the faculty club to watch a public television round-table discussion on multiple orgasm while her poor innocent students went off to the student union to munch hamburgers under a poster announcing an open-to-the-public round-table discussion on surgical sex changes. That's the trendy American way of sex—all science and liberation. Yet by and large I live amid chaste Americans, and I believe they are in the majority.

Sketches for a Novel to Be

Russian literature's notorious observatory power! The throat of a broken bottle (Chekhov). A swarm of gnats over the head of a marching captain second class (mine, and I won't let Chekhov have it).

The notorious West loves to play the coquette: I'm so bad, so decadent, so depraved. It pretends it doesn't give a damn about Russian literary observations and is in too much of a rush to pay attention to detail.

Sometimes a writer needs to fall into a trance and *stop* observing: everything's been whored and abhorred, sold twenty times over to "show biz" at the going rate. Even a classicist throws up his hands at the measures designed to suppress literary observation, East and West.

Write "A girl enters the room." That's enough. You think you ought to mention her rather British physiognomy: the slightly rounded forehead, slightly narrow features, the chin thrust slightly forward, the thick hair slightly skewed—but that interests no one; it is understood. After six months you may notice that the pupil of one eye (I forget which) has a tendency to spin wildly—but that has no relation to entertainment: it's your private life.

The chestnuts are no longer blooming, you'll say, and the prostitutes along the boulevard are lovelier than ever. But even these observations are unlikely to be of practical use; they are too blatantly situated in time.

The streets follow one another in strict consecutive order—Thirty-first, Thirty-second, Thirty-third . . . No one but you will be delighted by the fact that Beethoven Street flows between Thirty-third and Thirty-fourth; you might just as well have failed to notice it.

10

In mid-January, after a suffocating summer and long transparent autumn (both so unlike their Russian counterparts), Washington experiences a real three-week Russian winter of fierce blizzards and sudden ice-blue calms. On days like these an émigré couple wanders aimlessly through the numbered downtown streets, recalling the winter poems they used to read in school. The very air brings back Pushkin and the Ring Boulevard that encircles downtown Moscow.

Window-shopping. "Look, Maya! Good news! Smokings are on sale!" The poor benighted salespeople may be confused by the good Russian word *smoking* and will no doubt insist on calling the item in question a tuxedo, but the fact remains that Bertrand Russell Clothing is offering 50 percent off that most bourgeois of garments.

A moment of ideological vacillation at the door. Since the twenties and the days of the New Economic Policy, no one in the Soviet Union has played golf, eaten oysters, or worn "smokings," and so I find purchasing a tuxedo almost as fatal a step as emigrating. In the end, however, I am pushed across the threshold by antiideological logic.

No sooner do we get home than the phone rings. New York calling. "Mr. Aksyn . . . Mr. Aksen . . . Vassily! Would you care to attend our annual fund-raiser for the literary minorities of Canada?"

"Why, I'd be delighted. But tell me, how did you know to phone me just as I had reached sartorial maturity?"

"Ho, ho, ho! We aim to please. See you there!"

Next morning we awake to a howling blizzard. Visibility along the eastern corridor is close to zero. But the Metroliner races up to New York with a spirit not unlike that of the troika taking the hussar poet Denis Davydov from Moscow to Petersburg:

> *I'll sleep my way to Tver,*
> *In Tver get drunk with glee;*
> *To Petersburg, still drunk,*
> *I'll hie for one more spree . . .*

Looking out toward the Atlantic through the whirling snow, I ponder, as behooves an émigré, the vagaries of fate. As a fifty-year-old novice I was now becoming part of the mythical American literary scene.

ANSWERING AN ANSWER

The previous summer, on the way to our idyllic patch of Vermont, Maya and I turned off at Amherst, Massachusetts, where I had been invited to take part in a conference sponsored by the Theater Communications Group. Amherst's own idyll was in full bloom—a large village green bordered by chestnut trees and white spruce, squat little buildings with shops on the ground floor, and the church and halls of the college. The hotel where a room awaited us was called the Lord Jeffery Inn and reminded us of Stratford-upon-Avon.

We arrived toward evening. I turned on the television set. It was time for the news, and I wondered how the media would handle the event, which had begun that morning.

"Don't hold your breath," my wife grumped. "They don't call a theater conference news."

My wife takes a skeptical view of American television even though—or maybe because—she is an ardent follower of *Dallas* and *Dynasty,* shows that for many émigrés serve as an introduction to the language of Shakespeare.

"I don't know," I demurred. "It's not every day Massachusetts plays host to a forum of three hundred delegates from two hundred American theaters. And think of the celebrity value: playwrights like Arthur Miller, John Guare, Derek Walcott, Janusz Glowacki; directors Zelda Fichandler, Peter Sellars, Tadashi Suzuki, Liviu Ciulei . . ."

On flashed what Russians call "the blue screen." The first story dealt with race riots in the vicinity of Amherst. To us they looked more like a Russian brawl, the kind that results from one half of the village drinking itself cockeyed and ganging up on the other half.

Next came a long segment devoted to a fire in a small local hotel. Smoke, tongues of fire, a 300-pound male body bursting through a window and flopping, back first, into the tarpaulin stretched out below. Impressive footage! In Russia a fire is always a holiday. So Mother America loves a good fire, too.

There was no coverage of the theater conference—not on that evening or the next. What is more, during the three days of remarkably interesting discussion not a single reporter put in an appearance.

Actors from Tadashi Suzuki's school said that the first thing they did when onstage was to determine the point from which God's eyes were looking at them. Their lessons in stage movement earned them a standing ovation from the conference participants. Still, I thought, they'll have an easier time finding God's eyes than the eyes of the American public.

The lively and talented theatrical world of this country has had to take a back seat, to accept the role of a low-income relative. Where are the faces I saw at the conference, faces full of thought, imagination, humor? What the country sees in their stead, day in and day out, is screenfuls of personable nonentities with one message and one message only: to wooden mediocrity there is no end.

Someone (who? I wonder) had to lay down the unshakable aesthetic of "commercial" television. The director of the recent mini-series *The Sun Also Rises* justifies the violence he did to Hemingway by invoking the book's "impressionism." The impressionist approach, he says, would not stand up for a minute on commercial television. But what in God's name did he expect his work to say without the "impressionist approach"? That, if not for the Great War, Jake and Brett would have lived happily ever after? This kind of accommodation reduces an American classic to the level where we mistake an Estée Lauder commercial for the next scene.

The Soviet slogan ART BELONGS TO THE PEOPLE, though false in the land of its birth, has come curiously true in America. Since it is the mass audience that eventually forks out the cash, that audience ostensibly gets what it wants: the customer is always right. Yet what customers order depends on what they're offered. Unfortunately, those who do the offering tend to assume that people are "simple," and what they mean by simple borders on the simpleminded.

What people want depends on what they're offered. Essentially, then, the answer to the question of what people want is the answer to an answer. Mutual influence between mass audience and mass culture spins round and round in a vicious circle. Whose influence is primary? By now it is all but impossible to say.

No wonder the American avant-garde is in trouble. *Rolling Stone* reports that the reason the "Hollywood genius" Steven Spielberg was so long in receiving his first fat budget was that he was suspected of avant-garde tendencies. Poor Steven! He had to prove his purity.

A few years ago Paul Mazursky made a fine film, *Tempest,* which was not without its avant-garde romanticism—and which flopped at the box office: "the people," it seems, did not go for its complexities. Mazursky's next film, *Moscow on the Hudson,* was a comedy that managed to incorporate the tried and true canons of the soap. It was a box-office hit. What's a poor director to do when even Academy Awards are handed out on the basis of box-office receipts? In Moscow-not-on-the-Hudson we didn't call it "soap"; we called it, more crudely, "snot with syrup."

The clampdown on the avant-garde has been one of my great American surprises. From afar, from the empire of Socialist realism, we assumed that the avant-garde in America had continued to flourish, that the American cultural scene was a glittering, pulsating cosmopolitan playground. From within, I see with mounting astonishment that for all its scope, the American literary, theatrical, and cinematic establishment has certain traits in common with a general store: preference for the hot item, fear of risk, sheer panic at the thought of innovation.

Provincialism is not always a negative feature, of course, especially in literature. Faulkner is even more provincial than Dostoyevsky. Yet only now, living here, have I begun to grasp the degree to which American literature is American rather than international in essence. Now I see that, back in Moscow, our relationship to it depended on a kind of mythology.

Among the myths we accepted was the wondrous myth of the Famous American Writer (*znamenity amerikansky pisatel*) or ZAP, as we called him for short. In Moscow I was occasionally called upon to meet visiting ZAPs, and I thought I knew how to handle them. My wife, less experienced, still gets us in trouble now and then.

Recently a ZAP phoned us in Washington. He gave my wife his name and paused for the expected reaction.

"Would you spell that, please?" she said.

The flabbergasted ZAP, who had not been asked to spell his name by a fellow writer for thirty years, stammered his way through the letters.

When I came home, my wife said, "You had a call from an American writer whose name is . . . here, see for yourself." Her transliteration into Russian made it into something like Tutankhamen.

At that point the phone rang. "Mr.—uh—Axolotl? This

is . . ." The man gave his name, paused, and added, "The American writer."

"What!" I cried, trying to make up for my wife's gaffe with a show of enthusiasm. "Don't tell me *you're* the one who phoned!"

The ZAP gave a weary sigh of relief. "Yes, it's me."

At the dawn of my generation's literary existence, which to our great fortune coincided with the corroding of Stalin's iron curtain, five American writers captured the imagination of the young: Ernest Hemingway, William Faulkner, F. Scott Fitzgerald, John Dos Passos, and John Steinbeck—we called them the Great American Five.

I met only one. In the fall of 1963 John Steinbeck turned up in Moscow, a living legend in an ample coat, its pockets bulging with the essentials of any wandering ZAP: tobacco, whiskey, wire for tightening up plots, tackle for hooking metaphors . . . There he was, his broad face all wrinkles and alcoholic spider veins, one of the big ones of the century: cosmopolitan, vagabond, Don Juan, lush—in a word, "almost Hemingway." Even the Moscow police vaguely associated Steinbeck with Papa—to his obvious annoyance.

"I met your Hemingway," he told us, "only twice. The first time he paid for the Scotch; the second time I had to. We hardly talked. What was there for us to talk about? All he cared about was some titanic fish; the only fish I care about is the fish that will fit in a frying pan."

The American ambassador, Foy D. Kohler, invited me (no doubt as a representative of the "new wave" of Soviet writers) to a lunch in Steinbeck's honor. The legend must have had a few by the time I arrived for he greeted me with a clap on the back. "How's the writing going, Vassily?" I was thrilled. The hand of the ZAP!

He fit his image perfectly. All through dinner he talked a blue streak of fascinating gibberish to the horror of the diplomats and Alexei Surkov, secretary of the Writers' Union. "Why does man have a bellybutton? Well, if you feel like a radish in the middle of the night, friends, you won't find a better salt shaker!"

At a reception given by the magazine *Yunost (Youth)* he displayed a different side of himself. Scowling and sour, he lashed out at the young writers present with a set of obscure questions. "Don't you realize that the woods are on fire? Can't you hear the twigs snapping, the wolves howling? Will you fight for your skins or turn into a pack of mangy hounds yourselves?" Perhaps he was alluding to the crackdown on post-Stalinist art that the party had initiated not long before. The best response to his questions would have been Vladimir Vysotsky's famous song "The Wolf Hunt," but it was yet to be written. The darkness of the woods did not seem particularly relevant to the festival of our youth, which not even Nikita Khrushchev could spoil.

"Tell us about the times you met Hemingway, Mr. Steinbeck!" He fell scornfully silent. Then he asked for the toilet and disappeared.

Coming out of the *Yunost* offices into Moscow's dank late-autumn dusk, Steinbeck pulled his floppy hat down over his eyes, hailed a taxi, and growled and hissed to the driver the eminently growlable and hissable "Mar-r-r-ina R-r-r-osh-sh-shcha," his version of Marina Roshcha, an area of the capital known as a thieves' hangout. On the way he thought of how hard it was to be a Nobel laureate: always on display, never a moment to yourself. And these Russians! All they know is Hemingway, Hemingway. What makes this place tick anyway? Yevtushenko can't be the norm. Well, let's see what Marina Roshcha looks like, since I've been warned against it.

Although Marina Roshcha literally means "Maria's Grove," he naturally found no grove when the cab left him there. He walked toward the only neon sign, GASTRONOM, a place where Russians buy groceries and where, for want of bars, they gather to talk and drink. He'd heard of the widespread custom of three people each chipping in a ruble for a half liter of vodka. It always had to be three, but why?

And what was there about those mysterious cells of three that the police didn't like? He would have to look into the matter. Nobel Prize winners are not the kind to sip daiquiris under the Cuban sun; they go to the heart of the people, be it in North Dakota or Marina Roshcha.

He entered the swarming Gastronom and had a look around from his elevated vantage point. A man whose clothes had seen better days immediately recognized an accomplice when he saw one and, withdrawing a trembling index finger from inside his coat, gave him the sign. John held up his own sinful finger, and the two men started drifting together. A third, smaller, finger joined in, and out came the three rubles.

The bottle bought, they set off in high spirits, heads all but knocking, for a grimy little park. There the man who had seen better days took two glasses from his coat pockets: two of the men would observe the rules of etiquette; one would drink from the bottle. "Okay, big guy?" he asked Steinbeck. Steinbeck nodded and said, "Tell me, why do you always drink in threes?" "I've got an eye like a spirit level," said the smaller finger. "One hundred sixty-six grams for the two of us, and two grams extra for the big guy to grow on. Mud in your eye!"

After the first bottle the man who had seen better days pulled out a ruble that had seen better days; the smaller finger followed suit. The big guy, a.k.a. John Steinbeck, whipped out a ruble of his own. The second bottle went down smoothly, in tempo. "Will you bastards tell me why you drink in threes?" shouted John, pommeling his friends on their backs. "You talk too much," said the smaller finger. "The more you know the less you talk."

"Another round," said Steinbeck. The two Russians started scrounging in their pockets for spare change, but John produced three rubles of his own. "Big guy!" they cried out in amazement.

After the third bottle Steinbeck lowered himself onto an ice-covered bench and closed his eyes. "Bloody goodwill mission," he muttered, tuning out.

A jolt on the shoulder brought him to. There was a policeman standing over him demanding to see his *dokumenty.* An icy wind scraped through the branches. An odd customer, thought the policeman. Must be a foreigner.

Suddenly Steinbeck remembered two words his interpreter had taught him. "Amer-r-rikansky pi-s-s-satel," he said with a growl and a hiss.

Oh, an American writer, thought the policeman, saluting. "Welcome to Moscow, Comrade Hemingway!"

The moral of this popular Moscow legend is that even the Moscow police were to some extent aware of the ZAP phenomenon.

At the height of the Hemingway boom in the late fifties and early sixties, Papa was the idol of Russian students and intellectuals of all ages and persuasions. Even the "specialists" (read: KGB agents) poking around Cuba and South America fell under his sway.

The first time I saw Paris, in 1963, I found it beautiful not only for its thousand-year accumulation of elegance but also for the glimmer of those transient Americans of the twenties, the roistering crew of Lady Ashley's admirers. At the far end of the Boulevard du Montparnasse, where Marshal Ney's statue peeks through the chestnut trees, the strains of a piano float over from the Closerie des Lilas, I recalled whole passages of *The Sun Also Rises* and the magic of that unadorned prose.

The reason a Hemingway cult arose in Russia was that the author's lyric hero coincided with our idealized—and therefore false, though true, perhaps, in a certain astral sense—image of the American. The Hemingway hero epitomized what was so dramatically lacking in Russian society: personal courage, spontaneity, the willingness to take risks.

Vladimir Nabokov once dismissed Hemingway as a "contemporary Childe Harold." Quite accurate as far as it goes, but we must not forget what an impression Byron made on Russian society, especially on the aristocratic youth. The poetic genius of Pushkin and Lermontov had its roots in provincial Byronism; the Decembrist Uprising of 1825 was imbued with the Byronic spirit.

But there was another reason Hemingway seemed so attractive to us: his relation to alcohol. Russia's favorite vice needs periodic romanticization, the kind it received in the nineteenth century from Denis Davydov, a poet of wine, women, and much military bravado. Now Russia could drink with Hemingway in a new, American, cosmopolitan fashion. The alcoholic excesses of our generation owed a great deal to Papa's creations, and the dissipations of what would now be called our groupies would not have been the same without the escapades of a Brett Ashley.

Then, suddenly, everyone was exhausted; everything began to flicker and pale. And no wonder: Hemingway was a Renaissance writer, and when our Renaissance went up in smoke, the Hemingway cult went with it. *Hemminguyovina*, a word coined to designate the cult by the Moscow snobs who turned against it, has a scabrous, pejorative tinge to it, and the people who used it were also wont to say, "The tail of a Faulkner mule is worth more than all of Hemingway's blown-up bridges."

The time had come for a farewell to Hemingway. Farewell! I met you one night and you told me a simple little story about a "cat in the rain." Farewell, soldier of freedom! We shall never meet again in Pamplona nor drink straight from the wineskin. We shall never again drive our Jeep together through the deserted, German-free streets of Paris. We shall forget your lessons of love, the boat that keeps setting sail, the lore of buffalo shooting, of the sea, of sweat and Castilian mountain frost. Farewell, you can't come home, you're out of synch, hidalgo of the twentieth century, Childe Graybeard, farewell!

And having thus said my good-byes, I realize they are in fact a new encounter.

· · ·

Anyway, we're off to the literati party in New York. The snow is still coming down, whirling past Moscow style as our driver, by some miracle, lands us at our destination. He admits that he started driving a cab in New York only two months ago, that he's lived in New York only two months, and that he never expected to see anything like this cold, white sand that kept pouring out of the sky and made the roads so slippery.

Now I am standing in the crunch of a large gathering of intellectuals in downtown Manhattan. There is something of ancient Rome in these American stand-up parties. Someone always seems to be lurking about with a pair of daggers concealed in his toga. And Caesar? There he is, the author of something advertised as the crowning masterpiece of the age.

Unfamiliar faces by and large. Just one or two I remember from their visits to Moscow. Still, I'm in the heart of the literary establishment. I can feel it. All those tall women. Tall beauties, young and old. The process of selection has been going on for quite some time.

Suddenly I realize, not without a tinge of melancholy, that I'm not really interested in contemporary American literature. Suddenly I see my nostalgia go up in smoke. The cigarette smoke curling up from those tall women and the comfortably grizzled or balding pates of my American colleagues, the window embracing half the sky, the blinking hundred-story pillars of finance on the other side of the window—a rueful moment, the ebb tide of one of the joys of youth.

What went wrong? Either these people—and the ZAP image they personified—had changed radically since the old Hemingway days, or they never were what they seemed to us from afar, or I myself had changed with squeamish middle age, or the whole generation of Russian writers of which I am a part had changed radically after the Marxist medicine we had been forced to swallow . . .

Gone is the aura of far-off spaces, an open world, hazardous undertakings; American literature has simply taken its place in the ranks of Western literature as a whole. Now the aura of the hazardous undertaking belongs to the oppositional literatures of Eastern Europe and the Soviet Union. Where can a contemporary writer find a more vertiginous adventure than in literary exile?

Yet if I have lost my special interest in American literature, I have by no means written it off. On the contrary, I am full of professional curiosity, and as a member of the American Authors Guild I keep close watch on what is now, at least in part, my own professional turf.

My picture of the ZAP has changed oddly under the magnifying glass of American life. Writers everywhere are concerned with creating and perpetrating a public image. In the Soviet Union the Socialist Realist poet Sergei Ostrovoy, author of the immortal line "In Russia was I born, a mother bore me," will under no circumstances remove his thick glasses. "The people know me in these glasses," he intones. The ZAP is also concerned with his image. If bearded when first recognized by the critics, he will not shave; he clamps an unlit cigar between his teeth after he has come to hate it; having acquired the reputation of being a hermit, he lives like a hermit.

He's still the public's darling, your ZAP: a bit of a spoiled brat, a charming myth, and a stock character in American novels. A surprising number of fictional characters in current American fiction are authors. The neophyte writes a novel about a neophyte novelist. His first hit prompts a book about a first hit. Disillusioned with the glamour of fame, he writes about a writer's disillusionment. And with the advent of domestic disorders, betrayals, and adulteries comes a novel of a writer's betrayals, adulteries, and divorces.

The temptation is great. I know from experience. Every morning I sit down at my desk, look out over the rooftops of Washington, and yearn to write: "V. Axolotl, writer in exile, sat down at his desk and looked out over the rooftops of Washington." But I restrain my narcissism: mustn't set a bad example for the young!

The first commandment for professional writers is to move outside themselves. But when young American writers look at their older confreres and see them writing about their hemorrhoids, they naturally wonder, "Why can't I?" And so the *Atlantic*s and *Esquire*s of the land are littered with practically indistinguishable stories.

"Seated on her porch of a September evening, Sheila waited for her dinner guests. She was a slender 120 pounds and had a shock of thick, chestnut-colored hair, blue eyes, and rich hazel-brown skin, aglow with the tawny bronze light of the setting sun. [I ask: Is a setting sun always available?] Calmly and sadly she mused over her literary successes and the failures of her sex life.

"Her first book of stories had recently led to a sizable grant from the National Endowment, yet Bruce, who had just left her, had slept with her no more than twice a year during the five years they had spent together—10 times, all told. Other people slept together 10 times at one go, and every day at that, which came to 3,650 times a year or 18,250 times in five. What was the cause, she wondered, of our curious lag?

"An old Volkswagen pulled up, and out climbed her guests—Sheila's old college friend Jean [a second Sheila, no doubt] and Jean's boyfriend, Gordon [a third Sheila]. Just by looking at them she could tell they enjoyed the supersex of her calculations.

"The three of them made a green salad and ate part of it for dinner. That night Gordon came to Sheila and awakened the woman in her. [Any number of variants possible.]

"Next morning they had the rest of the salad and talked about literature. Sheila told of her plan to write a novel about a woman writer, Jean went on about the grant she was sure to receive from the National Endowment after her new book of poems came out, and Gordon shared his knock-down drag-out version of the Hollywood experience."

A few shifts in the crowd at the Manhattan party—a little distance from Caesar, a wider berth for Brutus—and I find myself next to a familiar face, a ZAP I used to read in translation and meet at international conferences. Now he complains to *me* about censorship.

"Yes, sir—censorship! You think only Russia has censorship. Do you know that not so long ago a local school board in Missouri ordered all my books off library shelves. It seems they're unhappy about some four-letter words and a few of my characters' shenanigans. Babbittry is back, I tell you. It's McCarthy all over again! And in the Soviet Union those books are translated and published!"

I scratch my head. "I think I can solve your problem for you. Have all your books retranslated into English from the Russian versions. I guarantee that the school board will find nothing in them to object to."

He looked up at me, a bit embarrassed. "Sorry, Vassily. I guess it was a little gauche of me to talk censorship with you."

After a college lecture one day a student asked me whether the leading American writers were well known in the Soviet Union. I prudently responded with a question of my own: Which writers did he have in mind? The student reeled off some names from the best-seller lists. What could I say? They were practically unknown to the Russian reading public. I myself had never heard of them until I came here. And although they are the ones who do the most to form popular taste, taste often seems the furthest thing from their minds.

The Russian reading public knows another American literature. Russian translators, to give them their due, select books for their merit, not for their sales. Of course, in those cases where ideology is an insuperable impediment, translators must not only trim their authors' hair but also gouge out bits of their flesh. Still, thanks to the generally high level of Soviet translations, Soviet readers in the last twenty-five years have had the benefit of a long list of brilliant American titles.

In the United States, meanwhile, the line between serious and popular literature has virtually disappeared. Sometimes a serious writer will make the best-seller lists; sometimes a glib habitué of the lists will tackle a difficult issue. By and large, however, the hunt for high returns produces both bad taste and stereotyped writers.

I once met a novelist who, when asked what kind of books he wrote, replied simply: "Best sellers."

"Unfortunately," he added, "they don't sell."

Literary hackwork bears a certain resemblance to ideological hackwork. Recently I heard a lady novelist reveal the tricks of her trade on a television talk show. Before writing a word, she said, she made a careful study of what was in demand. "A writer," she said, raising a well-manicured finger, "must know the literary marketplace." I have no trouble picturing that woman as a member of the Soviet Writers' Union. She has caught the high-minded tone: A writer must study the latest party documents and keep up with party resolutions on literary issues.

In its own oblique way, the American guild of best-selling authors is reminiscent of the Soviet party *nomenklatura*, the top reaches of the bureaucracy: it may be hard to join, but it is nearly impossible to leave. Often a book will become a best seller simply because it is written by a best-selling author. Readers trust the names on the best-seller list: they assume they are investing in a sure thing; writers, for their part, try to uphold their trademark. A kind of momentum builds up, a momentum serious literature is not immune to, either. And when that happens, good-bye experimentation.

I blame that same commercial momentum for the country's lack of interest in foreign authors. Umberto Eco's

Name of the Rose stands alone. As a bookseller once explained to me, "When the general reader leafs through a new book and comes up against 'difficult' foreign names, he automatically puts it down." Odd, isn't it, in a country where a good half of the population consists of John Dombroviches and Jane Giovannellis. In Russia, by the way, the situation is reversed; foreign names intrigue the reader.

It is also curious for me to see that literary criticism in America has so little effect on book sales. Rarely will the solid weeklies run a review of the latest blockbuster, and if they do it will be dripping with scorn and irony. Best-selling authors don't seem to need good reviews, however; they've made the list. The formation of literary taste takes place in a closed circle of people with good literary taste.

All things considered, though, I wish to pay homage where homage is due. To some extent I am now a part of this literature, a literature in which the Yoknapatawpha mule still flicks its tail, Spanish bridges still explode in the air, the beat generation plays it cool in jazz and life, and the wounded centaur of New England hobbles along his way. Whether literature suffers or gains from its cohabitation with the dollar is an open question. The sad fact is that the human race has failed to invent a system of economic relations more natural than money. What Karl Marx once proposed has turned into an attempt to reinstate a pre-monetary system. None of which deprives the writer of the right to use his claws. The face of the literary lion in the Piazza San Marco bids us to read; its claws bid us to write.

Digging itself "out of the rubble" of totalitarianism (the expression is Solzhenitsyn's), the Russian literary community—the Russian intelligentsia in general—counted on the solidarity of fellow artists the world over. In the sixties a number of the most brilliant talents of Europe were still under the influence of "progressive" circles, and any solidarity they had to offer went to the literary bosses of the various East-bloc writers' unions. Jean-Paul Sartre, for example, branded Pasternak a "troublemaker from the East" and declined the Nobel Prize, not wishing to follow in the footsteps of so reactionary a writer.

To their credit American writers rarely succumbed to the ideological hypnosis of the times. Hemingway's response to the Pasternak affair was more or less: If they kick Boris out, I'll buy him a house. Another sign of solidarity came from completely unexpected quarters, deep in the heart of Michigan. But that story requires a chapter to itself.

Sketches for a Novel to Be

Food for Generalization

Seven years ago in the city of Red Bluff, California, a worker in a lumber mill, a Mr. Hooker, abducted a twenty-year-old girl and kept her locked up as a sex slave. By day he stored her in a specially constructed box; by night he and his wife (they have two children) took her out, tortured her with matches, hung her from the ceiling, spread her out on a board, and "had sex" with her.

Generalization: They are all sex fiends.

The whole country is discussing the memoirs of Brooke Shields, *How to Maintain Your Virginity.*

Generalization: They are all purebred Puritans.

A Mr. Macfarland of San Diego, California, jumped onto the tracks to save his Irish setter from the wheels of an oncoming train. The setter survived. Mr. Macfarland lost a leg. "Some people call me eccentric," said the thirty-four-year-old bachelor, "but I don't think it's so crazy to sacrifice a leg for a loving, devoted, thinking creature. I get hundreds of letters from all over the country. Every one of them supports me. Most people love their pets more than we realize."

The generalization has been expressed by the subject (even though it is in wild contradiction to the laconic NO PETS addendum to 80 percent of FOR RENT signs).

11 One winter's day in the seventies an American landing force disembarked on the snow-covered paths of the writers' colony Peredelkino. Or so it must have seemed to the authorities when the head of Ardis Publishers, Carl Proffer; his wife, Ellendea; their children, Ian, Chris, and Andrew; Ellendea's brother Bill; somebody's mother, called "Grandma"; and two students, Nancy and Thais, appeared on the scene.

While the boys romped about in their brightly colored moon boots, Ellendea strode beneath the spruces with uncommon energy and verve, flapping her sumptuous, transoceanic mink creation open and shut, and Mr. Proffer (who had played first-string basketball for the University of Michigan in his day) walked along calmly, now and then lowering a slightly reddened nose into the scruffy, if not downright grubby, fur of his enormous Russian sheepskin coat. Carl was clearly enraptured: Russia, but not only Russia, Russian *literature* everywhere you look!

After *Metropol* came out and Socialist realism deprived the Proffers of the opportunity to return, they were no less stricken than many émigré writers. A unique brand of Russophilia, theirs: Michigan and Indiana born and bred!

Thanks to Carl Proffer a town called Ann Arbor, Michigan's "big little city," has gone down in the annals of Russian culture. It is a campus town complete with so-to-speak university Gothic, tiny restaurants, copy shops, late-night bookshops, student masses, a scent of marijuana symbolizing the liberal minority, fluffy pets darting among the domiciles of the stable majority, and streets with names like Hill, Spruce, Lake, and Elm, which a Russian writer drives past on his way to an unpaved road called Heatherway to find, half hidden behind a stand of oaks and pines, a large house—a former clubhouse—and the rolling hills of a golf course, where a tall, slightly stooped figure is walking two dogs and three children.

It was here that the Russian literary opposition entered a new stage. Miraculous "aerial ways" (to use Pasternak's phrase) connected this idyllic countryside with the kitchens of Moscow and Leningrad intellectuals, the garrets of Russian bohemia.

No American Slavist has understood the Russian literary scene the way Carl did. He was particularly skillful at detecting its "tough guy" aspect and even liked to put it on a bit himself. In any case, he was never one for high-flown proclamations or cold-blooded, academic deliberations; in fact, he got a kick out of breaking into an artistic string of Russian swear words now and then. Using this particular expressive device without going off the deep end demands special skill even from our own literary brotherhood: the line between playing with words and fouling the atmosphere is a fine one. Carl early acquired a feeling for Russian style extraordinary in a foreigner; he never lost it.

By the mid-seventies the Proffers had become full-fledged members of our lives. No one thought or spoke of them as the foreign patrons they were; they were always simply "the kids." "The kids phoned the other day; they're planning another trip." "The kids are thinking of putting out a complete edition of Bulgakov." And so on.

These two typical midwesterners penetrated so deeply into Russian culture that they sensed the faint but ever-present tension between the artistic communities of Moscow and Leningrad. Although they sought out descendants of Russian poetry's Silver Age among the canal dwellers of the north, Carl and Ellendea perceived the inroads that a certain provinciality had made on the former capital and noted a hint of the Smerdyakov mentality and of pseudo-classical pretensions there. Yet they never idealized Moscow, with its tendency to conformism, hedonism, and what we call bullshitism. Everything paled before their unbounded passion for Russian literature, which, according to the famous Ardis T-shirt, was "better than sex"—to say nothing of rock 'n' roll. Their love for the literature found a human focus in the great widows of our literature—Nadezhda Mandelstam, Yelena Bulgakova, Maria Platonova. Carl saw Joseph Brodsky as a fragile gladiolus from the banks of the Neva, Sasha Sokolov as a neglected fledgling of Nabokov's. Then the Ardis list was joined by Nabokov himself, a splendid iceberg with one Lolita above the surface and five Lolitas below. . . . Actually, none of this is quite true, but then it's not quite false either.

Once I saw Carl talking to two Moscow writers about having their books published. Next to their grungy, not-even-Levi's jeans look, he was the complete international literary promoter: pin-striped suit and stylish brogues, relaxed as a basketball player in the dressing room, yet eyes shining with a complete absence of the wheeling and dealing instinct—shining absence, hmm—and with a love not so much for the objects of that day's negotiations as for the cause holding us all together. It was a key moment: a talk with two sources of literature, an attempt to save them from oblivion, from exile underground.

Had Carl Proffer been a businessman first and foremost, he would probably have run his establishment differently—and run it into the ground. An item as unprofitable as Russian literature would have been smothered by the hard-sell approach; it needed other, more amorphous qualities: a combination of artistic temperament and university connections, unbridled enthusiasm, a feel for language, and something else—call it midwestern eccentricity, if you will.

I first heard of the Proffers from the literary dissident couple Lev Kopelev and Raya Orlova sometime back in 1971. At the time we were neighbors in one of the cooperative apartment houses for writers near the airport metro station in Moscow; now we are neighbors in exile—they live on the banks of the Rhine, I on the banks of the Potomac. They showed me the first issue of Ardis's *Russian Literature Triquarterly* and the first Ardis reprint (it was of Andrei Bely's *Kotik Letaev,* I believe) and raved, "They're really something, those American kids! They've set up a printing press in their garage and opened a publishing house! A couple of youngsters who teach at the University of Michigan! The boy's quite handsome, and that Ellendea—she's a real beauty!" In other words, our first news of Ardis was all exclamation marks. "A nice idea," I think I responded, never imagining that the "nice idea" would eventually offer a way out to a whole trend or, rather, a whole wave of contemporary Russian literature.

By then what has come to be known as the second or underground culture had established itself once and for all. Writers who had made their appearance as the thaw hastened to an end refused to go into hiding and bury their manuscripts in vegetable gardens; they gathered around bottles of cheap wine, recited their poems and stories at the top of their lungs, and proclaimed the emergence of new geniuses. And amid much bohemian graphomania some real talent did emerge: the poets Yevgeny Rein and Genrikh Sapgir, the novelist Venidikt Yerofeev . . .

Even official writers (of the "contradictory," that is, controversial variety) started collecting drawerfuls of "non-rot" material, material they felt ill suited to the rotten state of the nation and worthy of a different, more rational literary milieu. Many writers who had come to the fore during the height of the thaw, in the early sixties, were branded unpublishable. Let me cite my own case: Although I kept evolving as a writer, I moved further and further from official Soviet literature, filling my drawers with work; while on the surface I seemed to be on the wane—from full moon to half moon to crescent. . . . Andrei Bitov let his fine novel *Pushkin House* appear incognito and in pieces, that is, not as a novel but as a story here, an essay there, its core still hidden and waiting. Likewise Fazil Iskander carved off bits and pieces from his epic *Sandro of Chegem* to keep himself alive while he worked on.

There was only one way out: over the border or, as it came to be called, "over the hill." But publishing in émigré houses like Posev or its monthly *Grani (Facets)* (and later in the journal *Kontinent*) was tantamount to open confrontation with the regime, and only writers who had a political point to make were willing to take that route. If the purely literary underground tended to shilly-shally, it did so partly because it was just plain scared (and well it might have been) but partly because it was, consciously or unconsciously, disinclined to take a political stand, that is, because it tended by its very nature toward anarchy. The appearance of an independent, nonémigré, American, and not merely American but American university-based publishing operation whose basic concern was artistic quality alone provided the literary underground with a unique alternative.

Later, of course, when the *Metropol* affair was at its height, the watchdogs of Socialist realism pronounced Carl Proffer a CIA agent, a wily undercover man. Some people have a very simple view of the world: if it isn't KGB, it's CIA.

Now that our friend no longer roams the golf course, now that he has walked through the valley of the shadow of death, I see even more clearly that his contribution to Russian culture cannot be overestimated by the most superlative of superlatives. Anyone who takes a good look at the Ardis list for the first decade of its existence will understand what I mean. What matters is not so much the impressive number of titles as first, their very existence; second, the aesthetic and moral standards they set; and third, the appearance (in the "space" of Russian culture at the necessary place and time) of a figure willing to devote himself to a mission of artistic solidarity which, ludicrous as it is in comparison with today's vast ideological and commercial enterprises, has amply proved its worth.

I made my first visit to Ardis in July 1975 on the way back to Moscow from Los Angeles. I was still a Soviet writer. The house was jam-packed with young American Slavists and Russian refugees. New faces, glowing with emigration euphoria, turned up every day. True to Russian tradition, the kitchen served as a focal point for all-night discussions. Carl and Ellendea would laugh and say, "We're never quite sure how many people are staying here at one time. We go to bed and there are still, say, five people around the table; we come back the next morning and there they are—plus two or three more. We may put our two cents in, we may not: nobody pays attention to the hosts around here."

Even though the doors were always slamming, there were still children to be brought up, books to be brought out. Book production took place in the basement or, you might say, the basement was the headquarters of the perfidious undertaking that interfered in the Russian literary process without the approval of the Central Committee of the Communist Party of the Soviet Union. It was equipped with the latest in American small-scale technology—the various composers, printers, and copy machines that had conveniently become available or, rather, affordable at just the time Soviet literature was up in arms. Carl was terribly excited by the possibilities they represented. During one of our last phone calls—he was seriously ill at the time—he gave me a detailed description of a word processor that would read a manuscript, stop whenever it came to a problem, request an explanation, and then produce camera-ready copy.

In September 1977 the Proffers came to the Moscow International Book Fair and were not only admitted but even, wonder of wonders, allotted their own Ardis stand! Just before the doors opened I stood with Carl and Ellendea watching the crowd of Moscow bibliophiles growing, trembling in anticipation of the chase like a pack of borzois. The big-name publishers sauntered past the stand with a shrug of the shoulders. They didn't know what the Muscovites knew—that Ardis was unique: American and free, yet nonetheless Russian for it.

Permission had been granted for the display of English-language publications only, but at the last moment, with an agility left over from his basketball days, Carl packed the shelves with an array of Russian-language books: reprints of valuable works long out of print, new poetry and prose of internal and external émigré authors, and his favorite, hot off the press, a literary miscellany called *Glagol* (*The Word*). Suddenly the crowd started shouting the traditional "open at last!" and shoved its way toward the shelves. The looting was on. Books quickly disappeared into pockets and down shirtfronts. I saw one devotee who had clearly thought things out in advance: he was wearing outlandishly baggy trousers with rubber bands at the ankles and an elastic band at the waist and, totally unperturbed, dropping book after book into the seemingly bottomless pit.

No pillage has ever caused the pillaged such joy. Never before had I seen Carl quite so happy and excited. And never thereafter. His eyes shining, he kept piling *Glagol*s on the shelves. The intellectual looters were nonetheless exultant: books, books, and more books! It was as though Aladdin's cave had opened, the "holy boundaries of our native land" had opened! It was a rare moment of mass exhilaration.

Ardis was refused permission to exhibit at the next Moscow International Book Fair. Books became a prime concern of the border guards, and books—*Bücher, livres,* and especially Russian *knigi*—upset customs officials more than hashish or cocaine. Even so, the "Russian chain" was not broken; books migrated like birds, crossing the border westward in the form of manuscripts and returning between covers with the Ardis stagecoach logo. Once upon a time my two novels, *The Burn* and *The Island of Crimea*, landed at the Heatherway manor by this route.

When my wife and I landed there in person two months after leaving the USSR, Carl tossed me the keys to his Jeep and said, "Drive it as much as you like. Just don't forget to pay your parking tickets." He and Ellendea introduced us step by step to life in America, beginning, naturally enough, with a session on how to balance a checkbook. They were pleasantly surprised at how quickly we learned to cope with everyday things: renting an apartment, having a telephone installed.

"Tell me," I once said to them, "haven't you had enough of Russian literature?"

"More than you can imagine." They laughed, handing me an invitation to the reception they were giving to celebrate the Ardis publication of *The Burn.*

Long after we had left Ann Arbor, we kept up with each other on at least a weekly basis. Somewhere about midnight (the Ardis windows, like the windows of the Kremlin in Stalin's time, shone all through the night) the phone would ring and Carl would ask *"Kak dela?"* or "How are things going?" (our communications inevitably grew more anglicized from year to year) and give us the latest Moscow gossip, or we would exchange Soviet jokes fresh from their first stop in Paris or Copenhagen.

Whenever I heard his voice coming through the receiver, I thought of that night in January 1979 when the *Metropol* gang gathered round the shortwave radio in our Moscow kitchen to hear a fiercely jammed Voice of America interview with the head of Ardis. "We've just received a unique literary miscellany from Moscow," he said. "We don't know whether it will be published officially, but we intend to publish it in any case." Unlike certain émigré writers, who tried to pin ulterior motives on the *Metropol* initiative, our all-American immediately grasped its idealistic, literary essence.

In addition to everything else I simply enjoyed Carl's

physical presence, our periodic meetings in New York, Washington, Los Angeles, Milan, Paris, his head bobbing affably above the crowd. . . . The last time we saw each other before the onset of his tragic, heroic finale was at Rehoboth Beach, a Delaware resort town. A group of friends—Bob and Hannah Kaiser, Helen Yakobson, Maya and I—were relaxing with Carl and Ellendea on a balcony overlooking the ocean. Little Arabella, the Proffers' youngest, kept running up and making horrific cartoon-character faces at us. There was no hint whatever of the trials to come.

Several days later Carl was stricken with brutal pain. At such times I always recall Pasternak's lines:

> *My poems run, run on apace.*
> *I feel a greater need for you.*
> *Around the corner is a house*
> *Where the train of days has split in two.*

Carl Proffer was an exceptionally American, exceptionally university-oriented person and the way he died betrayed an exceptionally American and university-oriented—if I may call it such—"approach to the problem." He kept nothing silent and refused to speak in allegories. He said he wanted to live as long as possible so that little Arabella would remember him. He fought his disease for two years, undergoing several operations and several bouts of debilitating experimental therapy. In the intervals—and at times in a hospital bed—he would translate, write articles (a revealing feature on his battle with the disease for the *Washington Post* created a sensation), and work on his memoirs. He even made trips to Europe and the Caribbean.

Flying home from the Caribbean jaunt, the Proffers and their friends felt a sudden strong vibration. The passengers were requested to put on their life belts. How did their Anglo-Saxon, Scots-Irish panic register? Carl describes it as follows: "Cathy closed her eyes and started reciting her favorite poems; Len, a lawyer, worked out his will; Ellendea tried to finish the whodunit she was reading; and I comforted the woman on the other side of me, saying, 'Don't worry. The plane won't go down. Your neighbor here is on his way to another finale.' "

The illness seemed to emphasize his human qualities. His eyes had a gentle, kind sparkle to them. It was obvious he was enjoying every minute; every friendly chat was a gift from heaven, every glass of water a blessing.

And now he is gone. He was forty-seven, buried by his parents as well as his wife and children. Russian literature, American academia, writers the world over have lost a man of positive action so rare in our time of senseless hustle, when no one really listens, when books are skimmed rather than read and then only to provide clever repartee for votaries of literary lechery, when writers pound the keyboard day and night, obsessed with such high ideals as making next month's book club selection, raking in the royalties, grabbing up the grants, psyching out the Nobel, gratifying megalomaniacal passions, grasping, grasping, grasping, forming a clique of lickspittles, keeping the unknown and unpublished at bay, wallowing in endless and pointless interviews and presentations and public forums, raging for hours on the telephone, racing, racing, racing round a track with no start or finish, catching the attention of a readership brutalized by an unending stream of crap, resorting to the shock tactics of self-exhibition, or when policemen hoarse with ideological asthma exhort writers to wave the flag and create inspiring portraits of their contemporaries—in these absurd times we have lost one of the few men capable of direct and positive action, a man who taught students, wrote books, founded a publishing house worthy of its calling, and made the salvation of a humiliated and much maligned literature a cause to live by.

Sketches for a Novel to Be

1 9 8 o / The militant revolutionary Vladimirlenin Fidel-castro Karl Engels, wearing his Kazan University T-shirt, races his light-blue Porsche through wealthy neighborhoods at night. Keeping the bourgeoisie from getting a good night's sleep is his way of fomenting world revolution.

1 9 8 3 / A strange thing happens to the HMN. He is standing behind three Japanese women at TWA. "Here are our transit cards," they say in perfectly understandable English to the clerk behind the counter. The clerk gives them a pleasant smile and asks them to pay fifteen dollars each. The Japanese women don't understand and begin muttering among themselves in panic. "She says you must pay an additional fifteen dollars," the HMN graciously prompts. Suddenly the Japanese women are all smiles: so that was what she said! The clerk thanks the kind man for his help. The kind man is suddenly in panic himself. What language had he used with the Japanese women? He was sure it was Russian.

FOOD FOR GENERALIZATION

The car radio: "Our entire congregation is praying that the Wilsons will soon be over their plumbing problems . . . Traffic has slowed to a near halt for five miles beginning at Exit Twenty-seven . . . We pray that the Davises will survive their divorce . . . Mitch Snyder has completed a fifty-one-day hunger strike aimed at persuading the government to open another shelter for the homeless in the District . . . I wonder what the weather's like in Beirut, Ted. Is it like ours or worse? . . . A trailer and a truck have collided, scattering barrels of toxic material over the highway. There is talk of evacuating the local population . . . The Garden of Delights invites you to come in for a free pizza . . . A new hypothesis ties tornadoes with traffic on the right-hand side of the street . . . We pray for Lyndon Hook, who has begun renovations on his farm . . .

Generalization: *C'est la vie.*

12 St. Petersburg, Florida, is probably the strangest city we have visited in America. Dreary provincial streets, neglected houses, bumpy asphalt, and suddenly—a strikingly modern gallery with a good hundred canvases by Salvador Dalí. We had come to locate a monument to the city's founder, the Russian merchant Pyotr Dementyev. The first wave of émigrés, those who left Russia shortly after the revolution, never call the Florida town anything but Sankt Peterburg, thus keeping alive the name of their capital. (Renaming it Leningrad was like renaming Tolstoy Sholokhov.)

After dropping anchor here at the turn of the century, Dementyev changed his name to Peter Demens, and the monument we were trying to find, erected by the Congress of Russian Americans, was supposed to grace a pier called Demens' Landing. The locals we spoke to had transformed Demens' Landing into Demons' Landing and had neither heard of the Russian nor seen the monument. When we finally tracked it down, we understood why: it turned out to be a stone no larger than a suitcase and was all but lost among the sheltering palms.

To some degree the scope of that memorial reflects the state of Russian ethnic groups in America. Russian Americans lack powerful financial patrons, political lobbies, and Russian-language educational institutions. Their mainstay, the Congress of Russian Americans, makes itself felt most vociferously when protesting against the habit of the

American press to refer to Soviet functionaries as Russians.

And yet there are as many as two million Russians in America. In the years immediately following the revolution they made a considerable contribution to the development of society—Stravinsky in music, Sikorsky in aviation, Zvorykin in the development of television. If Russian Americans have been less keen than other ethnic groups to claim their ethnic due, it is largely because they have accepted the idea of the "death of Russia," that is, the irreversibility of the Bolshevik takeover.

The main unifying force is naturally the Russian Orthodox Church. In the Russian churches of New York, Los Angeles, Washington, Montreal, and Philadelphia we have seen genuinely Russian faces untouched by decades of Soviet deformation. We sometimes feel we have stepped onto the set of a film about prerevolutionary Russia.

The "Soviet deformation" all of us have undergone sets us off immediately from the local Russians. It shows in our walk and our gestures; it shows in our dress (which tends to be more Western than that of our Western fellow Russians) and, above all, in our speech, which has been sullied (though occasionally also enriched) by Soviet reality. You can tell a recent émigré from an old-time American Russian from the first few words. Once an elderly lady turned to us in a Connecticut Avenue crowd and said to us in Russian, "Hello! I couldn't help overhearing you speak Soviet." Of course our language is still very much Russian. As for theirs, it is in the best instance a beautifully preserved nineteenth-century textbook version of the same, in the worst instance a mishmash of Russian and whatever languages the speaker has picked up in his wanderings.

One day a group of Russian friends and I were shouting and laughing our way down a Washington street when some locals sitting on their stoops called out to us, "Hey, what language is that you're speaking?"

"Russian," we told them.

"Hmm." They shrugged. "Sounds too enthusiastic for Russian."

. . .

The Soviet press and Soviet literature early formulated their clichés about the Russian émigré. At worst he is a cynical White Guard villain, a traitor, an out-and-out scoundrel; at best, a down-and-outer, a derelict weeping into his rotgut over Mother Russia and her birch trees. As books from abroad began seeping over the border, we made up our own clichés: we imagined the Russian émigré to be fashioned more after the image of Vladimir Nabokov—writer, aesthete, lepidopterist extraordinary.

Needless to say, we have found no Nabokovs; we were naïve to presume they existed. The majority of the Russian Americans we have met are perfectly normal men and women. And, as might be expected, the older they are the more Russian they are, the younger the more American.

Old or young, however, they bear little relation to the bohemian Moscow-cellar or Leningrad-garret Russians of our avant-garde. For them Russian literature is still "I love the spring in early May" and "Go to the Volga, whose loud moan resounds." When an ex-Moscow artist tried to woo a Russian American mother of three away from her respectable Russian American husband, the gossips, pillars of morality in any society, were outraged not so much by the breakup of the family (which they see all the time nowadays) as by the intrusion of a decadent, a stranger, a *foreigner*.

One unpleasant discovery we have made is that certain of the less attractive aspects of Russia have been transplanted here and seem to be flourishing. Anti-Semitism, for example. Some local Russians still think that the Soviet Union is ruled by "those Jew Communists"; others vent their bile on the dissidents, claiming that the "Yids" are planning to ruin Russia again. Recently an American Russian Orthodox priest called on his parishioners to pray for the salvation of Yelena and Andrei—Yelena Bonner and Andrei Sakharov. When a group of older women in the congregation protested against "praying for kikes," the priest, an enlightened and profoundly religious man, was so taken aback that his first response was to explain that only Sakharov's wife was Jewish . . .

People who think like those women are in the minority and dying out. Most members of the postrevolutionary and postwar waves of emigration have accepted the new wave. As one of them puts it, "You new arrivals have been a breath of fresh air. Thanks to you, we American Russians have come to realize that being Russian doesn't necessarily mean being musty and backward."

THE THIRD-PERSON "WE"

After a few years in America we have begun going through the stages the older émigrés have long since outgrown. One such stage seems at first more grammatical than existential: it involves the use of the pronouns "us" and "them."

"It's a disgrace what we're doing in Afghanistan! . . . Why did we go and shoot down that Korean passenger plane? . . . The Americans are beating us in space . . ." It was only natural: "we" hadn't changed; "we" was still we Russians, we Soviet Russians.

As time went on, however, we began to change and "we" began to change: we began to change from Soviet Russians into Russian Americans; "we" began to change from the first person to the third. In grammar as in life, periods of transition can be nerveracking.

I look up from the newspaper and say to Maya, "Look at this. There's been another spy exchange in Germany. They're handing over four for twenty of ours."

"Why, that's terrible!" she fumes. "When will they learn to negotiate with us!"

Total confusion. My "they" refers to the Soviets; her "they" to the Americans. I meant the exchange was to the advantage of the Americans; she meant she regretted it was to the disadvantage of the Americans. Finally we made a deal: "Their our are no longer our ours, and our ours are ours, okay?"

On we stumble toward Americanization, gradually coming to grips with what it means to be more than exiles, to be Russian members of the Western bloc.

"CHRIST IS RISEN" IN D.C.

Orthodox Easter, a movable feast, coincided recently with Western Easter and Passover. We enjoyed being able to share the holiday with the whole city and looked forward to the midnight service at our humble church, St. John the Precursor.

There are two Russian Orthodox churches in the city. At St. Nicholas's the priest, Father Dmitry Grigoriev, a professor of Russian literature at Georgetown University, conducts the service almost completely in English. We naturally chose St. John's, the church where the service is in Russian. Our priest, Father Victor Potapov, is a lively, pleasant man in his early thirties, who has devoted his life to the Russian church. Born in America, he has a fine knowledge of Russian (it is hard to believe he spoke Russian with an accent when he was younger) and Russian literature (classical, émigré, *and* Soviet). His sermons are uplifting in both style and content, and his house in Silver Spring, presided over by his wife, Masha (we can't quite bring ourselves to use the traditional designation for a priest's wife, *matushka,* with the young and pretty Parisienne from the famous Rodzianko family), is the scene of many joyful, noisy holiday evenings. Like many other members of the parish, we consider ourselves friends of the family.

Anyway, we arrive at St. John's just before midnight. The belfry and cross are lit. Since the church can't accommodate all the Easter worshipers (attendance runs as high as four hundred), the steps of the church, then the slopes of the hill it rests on are soon filled with Tolstoy- and Chekhov-like faces flickering in the flames of their candles. For some reason Easter nights are always windy here.

At midnight the bells ring out and the procession of the cross makes its appearance. It is headed by a group of children including Seryozha and Mark Potapov and Philip, the five-year-old son of the writer Sasha Suslov. As they pass by, I hear them whispering to one another in English. (Although they can speak and even read Russian, they find speaking English more natural. Passing on the language is a difficult task. Ads for summer Scout camps in Russian newspapers announce plaintively, "We accept children with even minimal Russian.")

"Christ is risen from the dead, conquering death with death," the choir intones. *"Khristos voskres!"* Father Victor proclaims. "Christ is risen!" *"Voistinu voskres!"* the congregation responds. "Verily He is risen!" Lord, we can't help thinking, so many Russians and a total lack of Marxism-Leninism! The traditional triple kisses begin.

American TV now shows scenes from Easter services in Moscow. Despite the presence of a huge number of militiamen and "people's volunteers" (or because of it), everything seems quite dignified. What I recall is huge crowds of half-drunk, uncomprehending adolescents knocking down churchyard fences. Perhaps after nearly seven decades of militant atheism Russians see the meaning of Easter as a protest against Marxist primitivism. The next step is for it to turn back into a normal, joyous holiday, the kind we celebrate in Washington.

THE NEW RUSSIAN TRIBES

Having spent all their lives as suspect foreigners on their native soil, Russian Jews have moved to New York, Los Angeles, and of course to the land of the Bible to discover that they are in fact Jewish Russians. In both America and Israel they are called "Russians" no matter how "Jewish" their names, no matter how curly their hair, no matter how prominent their noses, and no matter how guttural their r's. They could not be officially Russian in Soviet Russia because their internal passports designated them as Jews; they had to leave to become Russians.

The émigrés do not consider their "new Russianness" a marvelous acquisition or an object of particular pride: the marvelous acquisition is the right to be proud of their great Jewish heritage. But the new Russianness is a fact, and it goes more than skin deep.

In old Russia the spirit of the Jewish community centered on the synagogue. Forcibly cut off from the synagogue and its language and culture for several generations, the new arrivals often disappoint the American Jewish religious organizations that did so much to release them. Many think of themselves as Jews in name only and could not understand why they were constantly being dragged to services. If American Jews were surprised by their coreligionists' lack of Jewishness, they were absolutely bewildered by the intellectuals among them who had participated in the unofficial Soviet "religious renaissance" of recent years and emerged from their homeland as Buddhists and Krishnas, as followers of Madame Blavatsky and Monsieur Gurdjieff, but most of all as—Christians, Orthodox Christians. To some extent even the residents of Little Odessa head for Russian churches at Eastertime to have their *kulichi*, their Easter cakes, blessed.

Another interesting "reverse phenomenon" is that of cultural nostalgia. Once upon a time they chased after American films; now they chase after Soviet ones. A TV show on the life of the émigrés shows a group of elderly people watching an old Soviet war film on a VCR, wiping away their tears to the strains of "The Girl Went with Her Soldier to His Position." And Moscow is apparently abreast of the situation. How else could the latest films reach émigré communities all over America, sometimes with guest appearances by "stars of the East bloc"?

A few years ago the émigré press launched a campaign against a tour of Soviet variety show performers. Groups of activists picketed the concert halls. To no avail. The audience hadn't the slightest interest communism, Marxism, or any ism whatsoever; it simply wanted to see its Russian idols.

No one boycotts the idols any longer. A treacle-voiced crooner elicits mass sobs from former Odessites and Minskers with a song about swans in love. Yevtushenko shows a three-hour self-indulgent film about his childhood, and the new tribes greet him with delight. Again, the furthest thing from anyone's mind—from the minds of the audience, the singer, and Yevtushenko, for that matter—is Soviet communism. The appeal is purely Russian.

An even more eloquent indicator of Russian patriotism is gastronomy. I have mentioned the search for the pot-cheese-like *tvorog,* but let's not forget the various kinds of sausage—soft, medium, hard, and so on—whose "qualities and quantities" had undergone considerable corrosion during the recent years of "mature communism"; let's not forget mushrooms, the pride of many a Russian table; let's not forget chocolate-covered cherries and Turkish delight. The new restaurants the émigrés open tend to fall into time-worn Russian patterns: Sadko, Metropole, National, Ruslan, Kalinka, Sankt Peterburg. Ditto the bands that play there and the brawls that break out there.

Thanks to the unlimited capitalist marketplace the new Americans (or is it new Russians?) can satisfy their immediate national nostalgias more readily than their ancestral religious ones. Some understandably regret the assimilation of these Jews, the loss of ties with an ancient cult and culture; others see it as evidence of how nations can live together despite provocation and prejudice. Together Russians and Jews made the revolution, together they went into the war and the gulag, together they built their nauseating socialism, and together they recoiled from what they had wrought.

Open a copy of the New York Russian daily *Novoye Russkoye Slovo,* and you will see obituary notices like the following side by side: "The Union of Elders of the Kuban Cossack Company and Officers of the Armored Train George the Victor announce with profound sorrow that by the will of God, Cornet Fyodor Ivanovich Yegorov passed away in his ninety-fifth year on such and such a date" and "On such and such a date after a prolonged illness our much beloved Berta Finkelstein was taken to her maker. She had a big heart. She leaves relatives in Brighton Beach, Haifa, and Odessa."

Of course you can smile and say, "Oh, the irony of fate." Or you can pray for two departed souls.

Sketches for a Novel to Be

1 9 8 3 / When you run, no one touches you. No one needs you when you're running. Every fool knows you're only worth a handful of sweat. Just keep running. If I'd kept running, I wouldn't be in this ridiculous situation.

Such are the thoughts of Russian runner Lyova Groshkin as he stands with a gun pointed at him on dark Santa Melinda Street near the Professor Devonshire's widow, where he paid symbolic rent on an alcove, wardrobe, and shower. The wardrobe, incidentally, held some rather fine clothes belonging to the late professor, and his widow, who adored her silent, smiling Russian of a roomer, did not mind his wearing them. Perhaps it was the tweed jacket that caused three practicing revolutionaries to aim their big gun at him.

"Your wallet, man!" says the leader. "Fork it over."

"Sorry, guys, but I don't understand English," Lyova responds, in Russian, smiling his international youth smile at the revolutionaries.

Although the muzzle jerks ever so eloquently and the modulations of the voice behind it are totally convincing, Lyova fails to understand. He really doesn't understand English.

"Hand over your money, your watch, your rings. Give me everything you've got, you motherfucker, or I'll blow you up on the spot!"

"Can't you understand I don't understand?" Lyova is

getting angry. "Fuck off, will you!" And he turns and walks off, wondering how to control his adrenaline enough to keep his shoulder blades from twitching. He'd have to work on that.

There is no shot in the back. The revolutionaries realize they have made a mistake. They thought he was a middle-aged bourgeois in a tweed jacket, but he'd turned out to be one of them. Young and decked out in "borrowed" clothes.

13 During my five years in America I've been to some fifty campuses, including Berkeley, UCLA, Stanford, Sonoma State, Irvine, Santa Cruz, Occidental, the University of Washington, Indiana University, the University of Michigan, the University of Kansas, Oberlin, Vanderbilt, Miami University, Ohio State, the University of Virginia, the University of Richmond, Columbia, CUNY, Hunter, Amherst, the University of Maine, Dartmouth, the University of Chicago, Boston University, Norwich, Middlebury, Sweetbriar, Princeton, Georgetown, George Washington, Johns Hopkins, and Goucher. Many a quad has doubtless supplied fertile grazing land to Irony the Cow, but, all things considered, American universities represent a fine, positive, bracing force in American society.

The very idea of a "campus" as a miniature autonomous unit within the colossus of the state is both incongruous and encouraging to an East-bloc émigré. Several of the oldest universities in Russia (including my alma mater, Kazan) have retained a few purely territorial traces (a fence, a gateway) of autonomy, and there was a time when the liberal press would squawk if the local police so much as set foot on the premises. But no Soviet student has ever dreamed of "campus life" in the American sense. First of all, Komsomol pressures and general discipline are ferocious. Then, as virtually all institutions of higher learning are dispersed throughout large cities, students must use means of public transport to get from one lecture hall to another. But most important, the juxtaposition of "university" and "autonomy" sounds positively oxymoronic.

It never occurred to me in the Soviet Union to stand in front of a classroom and enlighten the minds of the young: writers have no place in the Soviet university system. But even if they had, my general reputation, which degraded during the seventies from "writer given to contradictions" to "subversive element," would have made me anathema to the educational authorities.

The writer is as common on American campuses as the cocker spaniel in the American home. Any school worth its prestige needs one or even two of them to ennoble the educational atmosphere with his creative presence, add the raisin to the dough (as we say in Russian) or the paradox to the cocktail party (as you might say in English), that is, to add a bit of spice, a bit of eccentricity to the general run of faculty members. In practical terms, the writer-in-residence plants himself on the lawn, his mouth half open (or, better, sporting a pipe), his gaze fixed innocently (in theory, that is) in front of him.

Who comes out ahead of the university/writer symbiosis? I gain a monthly salary, which pays the rent for a Washington apartment. But the university gains as well. If Goucher College, where I am in my third year as writer-in-residence, wishes to place a major advertisement for itself in the *Baltimore Sun,* it must fork out a sum exceeding my yearly salary; every article about me or my works earns their institution a free plug.

Apart from pecuniary considerations, however, I'm not sure what effect my presence—or the presence of my wife or, for that matter, our cocker Ushik bounding across the campus with unwieldy sticks in his mouth and basking in the students' admiration (what do you expect from the dog of a writer?)—has on campus life. All I can say is that the most important effect it has on me is the surge of high spirits I feel whenever I'm in the midst of a happy, healthy, openhearted, and open-minded group of young people.

MY MARYLAND AMAZONS

Goucher College, one of the few remaining sex-segregated colleges in the country, has a student body of a thousand young women. The president, the historian Rhoda Dorsey, is naturally a woman, and all male members of the faculty are naturally convinced feminists.

Because America is so much younger than Russia, it has been deprived of historical assets like two centuries of Tatar raids; it boasts no skirmishes with Teutonic knights on frozen lakes or with the Swedish Navy on the high seas. But in matters of university education we are, historically speaking, more or less equal: most Russian institutions of higher learning, like their American counterparts, are of much more recent vintage than the great West and Central European universities. In other words, the fact that Goucher has recently celebrated its centenary is as impressive to Russian as to American ears.

The campus is located on the Beltway that encircles Baltimore, about an hour and a quarter commute from my place in the District. By way of a plug I might point out that it consists of 340 acres of woods, fields, and parking lots, to say nothing of lecture halls, an observatory, and an ecumenical chapel (which can accommodate any rite but Leninism, because Lenin maintains permanent quarters elsewhere). It also has a gymnasium and pool, playing fields for field hockey and lacrosse, six tennis courts, and a stable and show ring.

By the way, the students look smashing on horseback; the horses look pretty smashing, too, with their graceful young Amazons. Another Amazon connection: the most popular sport at Goucher is archery. But there all similarity with the female warriors ends. We have noticed no hostility whatsoever toward the once stronger sex. Thanks to a consortium with neighboring Johns Hopkins, we have more than an occasional male student in our classes, and in the shuttle connecting the two campuses the battle of the sexes is frequently resolved in a manner that is anything but academic.

I've mentioned the alarmist side of American statistics before. Well, try this one on for size: "One in every ten American students is an alcoholic." Believe me, during all the lectures I've given across the country, during all the classes I've taught, not once have I seen a student "drunk" in the sense the word has in France or Germany, let alone Russia.

Throughout my student years in Kazan and Leningrad I was involved in serious fights. We fought over girls at dances, we fought over football or hockey matches, and (most often) we fought over nothing at all. We fought one on one, we fought in gangs, we fought class against class, department against department, school against school. I remember the time traffic came to a halt along broad Stone Island Prospect as a result of a monumental battle between the College of Mines of Leningrad State University and my school of medicine; I remember the time the electrical engineers waded their way across the municipal canal to make a surprise attack on a ball being given by the mechanical engineers.

Never have I seen anything vaguely similar in American universities. In fact, it's hard for me to imagine my students—or, rather, their parents—going so far as to demonstrate or burn an effigy or two. American students (at least today's American students) are extremely well bred young men and women. Our Goucher girls do not differ too greatly from the young ladies who attended the liberal Smolny Institute for Daughters of the Nobility before the revolution, a school that, unfortunately, after the revolution became a dormitory for Bolshevik commissars. Let us hope that history does not repeat itself on the northern edge of Baltimore along Route 695.

In my search for the "Russian Room" I pass through a student dormitory. My presence in these hallowed halls causes a wave of panic. Some doors slam shut; others inch open to reveal a nose and a pair of eyes; a scantily dressed figure darts from one room to another in a flurry of pink, rounded extremities. "There's a man in the dorm, girls!" A man in a trenchcoat appearing out of nowhere and therefore mysterious, with mustache and pipe in the glass door in front and scarf and umbrella in the glass door behind. I don't know whether to be embarrassed or flattered.

Then out pop two punks—one purple head, the other green.

"Good day, good sir," they say, their particolored curls shaking with excitement. "Might we interest you in a drive to the Trident?" I mumble an indefinite thanks for the invitation, next time perhaps, when I'm a bit more mature. Suddenly all the doors fly open. Everyone is calm and collected. "False alarm, girls! It's just Aksyonov, our writer-in-residence." Whereupon I hunch along the wall like Updike's centaur . . .

Yes, all those sexual and drug revolutions notwithstanding, American students are amazingly genteel, pure, even (stone me, if you will) chaste. Oh, I may catch a whiff of grass now and then, but I smell popcorn a lot more often. There may be no taboo topics in the classroom, but in life traditions go unflouted. The air seems as full of unabashed romantic love as in the early chapters of *War and Peace.* In fact, I would venture to say that the average Komsomol girl has a good deal more dissipation under her belt than our average Amazon.

What makes American students major in Russian? The hard-boiled among the Soviet party ideologues believe they have the answer (and they quickly believe their own lies). They see American Russian departments as branches of the CIA and tend to choose scapegoats among the faculty—Maurice Friedberg of the University of Illinois and Deming Brown of the University of Michigan have been particularly susceptible lately—to hate with every fiber of their bodies. (I can just imagine Albert Belyaev, known in Moscow as "Cobblestone—Weapon of the Proletariat," fuming over the works of these perfectly respectable scholars because they shun the Marxist approach and treat works and authors on the Soviet index.) That some graduates of American Russian departments do enter the ranks of intelligence is only natural, but the percentage is infinitesimal. Enrollment in Russian-language courses varies widely from decade to decade, and it is all but impossible to tell what accounts for the variation. Is it the cold war, Sputnik, détente, the recent cultural emigration, exchanges, tours, marriages? In any case, the number of Russian students in the country appears to be on the rise.

Russian émigrés have traditionally found refuge on American campuses. Is there any finer refuge from all the executions, revolutions, prisons, and escapes than the one Nabokov describes in *Pnin* as "a somewhat provincial institution characterized by an artificial lake in the middle of a landscaped campus, by ivied galleries connecting the various halls, by murals displaying recognizable members of the faculty in the act of passing on the torch of knowledge from Aristotle, Shakespeare and Pasteur . . ." With the new wave of emigration, Nabokov's absentminded Professor Pnin has made a comeback on American campuses.

If I have managed to escape complete Pninification, I have done so not so much by being careful to take the right lectures to class as by not putting all my eggs in one basket. In fact, I first turned to the university because I felt it would make less of a dent in my writerly day than any of the alternatives. Little by little, however, I found I was deriving a new kind of enjoyment from teaching, and the more I thought about it the closer I came to the tritest of conclusions: that I found teaching, yes, rewarding.

When you get down to it, the subject I teach, contemporary Russian literature, is light-years away from American college students' everyday concerns. Even the most intellectual among them, those who have a vague idea about it, treat it as deserving of pity: "Sure, it's full of noble emotions, it means well, but what a drag, reading about the . . . well, the insulted and the injured all the time." My job is to show that for the last three decades the Russian literary scene has been alive and kicking in a way unknown to these shores.

Here are the main landmarks in one of my first seminars ("Existence = Resistance"): the thaw of 1956 and the miscellany *Literary Russia* as a revolt against literary Stalinism. The Pasternak affair and the Nobel Prize. The journals *Novy Mir (New World)* and *Oktyabr (October)* as antipodes in the spiritual battles of the sixties. The founding of the journal *Yunost (Youth)* and its role in furthering "young prose." The transformation of "young prose" into open nonconformism. Poetry fever and its superstars. Samizdat. Samizdat on tape. Guitar-strumming bards as symbols of resistance. The Solzhenitsyn affair and the Nobel Prize. The expulsion of Solzhenitsyn. The exodus and further expulsion of writers. Tamizdat (publication of forbidden works abroad for the purpose of smuggling them into the country). *Metropol* as a last-ditch attempt to break through the ideologists' lines. Emigration.

When I talk to the offspring of the American suburbs—a country of its own, a country of riches and well-being within the country—when I talk to them about Soviet reality (in terms of my old friends and what happened to them) and watch their picture of Russia changing from a vast dark blob on the map to a battleground for human dignity in the face of brazen totalitarian power politics, I realize the university is not simply a retreat or the source of a monthly paycheck; I realize I am doing something eminently worthwhile.

It is the first day of classes. The secretary greets me with discouraging news: "Only one student has signed up for your graduate creative writing course. Oh, and she can't come today because she's marrying one of the professors."

"Well, well," I say to the secretary. "I hope our lucky colleague won't object to my one-on-one meetings with the blushing bride." Actually, of course, I'm furious: If they don't want to know anything about Russia, so be it. I proceed to the standard generalizations: *they* don't care about the outside world. Finally I wander over to the classroom—just in case—and find twenty students waiting eagerly. The computer has made a mistake.

"Future writers of America! What do you know about contemporary Russian literature?" The answer? Nine male smiles, eleven female smiles. "Not a thing."

"Well, then, can you at least name a contemporary Russian writer?" Anything to start off the discussion.

More smiles. More silence. At last an eyebrow twitches. "I don't know if I can pronounce it correctly." An approximation of Solzhenitsyn follows.

Not that I had any great expectations. I just couldn't help grieving to learn that college graduates in a master's creative writing program had never heard of Akhmatova or Pasternak (though when I mentioned his name another eyebrow went up: "Oh, you mean Julie Christie and Omar Sharif—wait, what was the name of that movie? . . . Right! *Dr. Zhivago*") or Mandelstam or Bulgakov or the superstars Yevtushenko or Voznesensky, to say nothing of Akhmadulina, Iskander, Trifonov, or Bitov.

True, they had heard of me. That spring *The Burn* was all over the bookshops and I was in all the major newspapers. That was why they had signed up for my class.

"Aren't you a little ashamed of yourselves?" I said by way of admonition. "A little," they said by way of agreement. But I could tell they weren't, not in the slightest.

Let me cite an example from another field. A couple of years ago I opened a newspaper to find a picture of an old Moscow friend, the extraordinary film director Andrei Tarkovsky. He had just defected to the West. Well, I thought with a chuckle, at last Americans will have to recognize one of our geniuses. But the text accompanying the picture brought me back to reality. "Tarkovsky," it said, "is a famous Soviet director. In 1962 his first film won the grand prize, the Golden Lion, at the Venice Film Festival. Since then he has received numerous other international awards. He is totally unknown in the United States." Is that arrogance or ignorance?

The American public (and here I may expand my generalization to include the entire Western public) cultivates a curious kind of snobbery. Prove it ignorant of something and it will counter by asserting that your "something" is simply not worth its attention. Not only did my students feel no shame at their ignorance of contemporary Russian literature; they felt that contemporary Russian literature had to be flawed because they were ignorant of it.

There's too much of everything, I tell myself, too much information, too much hype. But snobbish ignorance in the face of shampoo brands is one thing; snobbish ignorance in the face of contemporary Russian literature is something else. Thinly disguised provinciality.

The snobbish smiles soon vanished in my classes: once the students started reading, they realized what they had missed. The fault is not theirs. No one had ever told them about it before; no one had made them see that not knowing recent Russian literature was the same as not knowing recent American literature.

The topics we discussed included how the creative impulse arises, what makes a writer write, at what point mind takes over from emotion, how fact and fiction intermingle. I was able to contribute a good deal more than my own hunches thanks to a questionnaire I had distributed in 1975 among a group of colleagues (who blithely proceeded to contradict one another and themselves). Major writers all—Bella Akhmadulina, Andrei Bitov, Andrei Voznesensky, Anatoly Gladilin, Yury Nagibin, Fazil Iskander, Valentin Kataev, Yury Trifonov, Anatoly Naiman, Bulat Okudzhava—they were *terra incognita* to the class, but I was amazed at how swiftly its viewpoint shifted. In the very first set of papers, that is, only two weeks into the semester, I noticed a budding sophistication.

Peter took on Iskander's novel, *Sandro of Chegem,* an unfinished (that is, ongoing) and rollicking epic set in the author's native Abkhazia, a tiny place Peter had never heard of before. And suddenly here he is, an instant expert, informing his classmates that Abkhazia is located on the east coast of the Black Sea in the foothills of the Caucasus and is actually the land to which Jason and the Argonauts set sail in quest of the Golden Fleece, that Iskander belongs to the great Mediterranean culture of which Homer was a part and his *Sandro* represents a late modern development of the early modern picaresque genre, that literature in Russian by and about members of a non-Russian ethnic group has its own specific features and problems, and—oh yes—and that it would not be amiss to erect a metaphysic of Stalinist infamy on the basis of the work . . .

Susan unearthed a few British translations of Kataev and came to class raving about him. Kataev, now almost ninety, may be all but unknown here, but like so many other excellent contemporary Russian writers he has been translated and is therefore—theoretically, at least (in other words, wherever there is a decent university library)—available. While delving into the twenties, Kataev's "golden years," Susan discovered Mikhail Bulgakov and went on to develop an original theory, namely, that the young writers of the twenties wrote, in part, to overcome the claustrophobia of Soviet life.

By the end of the semester the students were calling Akhmadulina "Bella" and comparing her metaphors with those of Tsvetaeva and Akhmatova, entering into the minds of Bitov's cerebral heroes, finding their way through Trifonov's Moscow, sounding out Voznesensky's cosmic connections, and subjecting Yevtushenko's berries to minute inspection.

We devoted one of our last sessions to a discussion of

whether Russian literature has a future. Chris started the ball rolling by pointing out that "unlike many major languages of the world—English, French, Spanish, Portuguese, German, and Arabic—Russian is spoken within the bounds of a single state, a state, moreover, that is totalitarian in ideology and can therefore subjugate literature to its own needs."

"True," said Liz, "but given the new wave of emigration Russian literature also has room to evolve freely. The works I find most appealing are the ones being written outside Russia. For the time being—for the rest of the twentieth and even into the twenty-first century—the center of Russian literature may well have shifted from the mother country to the diaspora."

"But can a diaspora produce a true national literature?" George objected. "And isn't it likely that after a generation or so Russian literature outside Russia will simply cease to exist? Think of the factors working against it: writers cut off from their language, writers forced to make a living outside literature (sorry to bring up something so prosaic). But most of all, the pressure to assimilate. It's extremely strong, you realize, especially in America and Israel, where most of the émigrés have settled. The toll on the second generation is bound to be enormous. As for the third generation, you'll be lucky if it can *read* Russian much less write masterpieces in Russian."

"Now let's think of the factors working for it," said Patrick. "Some literatures—Jewish literature, or Armenian—have withstood the trials of the diaspora for hundreds of years. Besides, the number of Russians currently in exile is enormous. More than the population of England during the time of Shakespeare. And the percentage of intellectuals—that is, readers—in their number is extraordinarily high. Next argument. The current group of émigrés represents 'the third wave.' The first came after the revolution, the second after World War II. Who would have predicted this wave, and who's to say the Soviet Union won't accommodate us with more?"

"There are other factors as well," Hugh pointed out. "Émigrés aren't the only ones who read émigré literature. A decent émigré writer can usually count on having his works translated into the language of the country he has adopted, and if they do well translations in other languages will follow. Besides, books by émigrés are regularly smuggled into the Soviet Union, and a single copy, circulating clandestinely, can reach hundreds of readers. When an émigré author is read (or reads) over a Western radio station broadcasting to the Soviet Union, his audience runs into the thousands and tens of thousands. Tape was the innovation of the sixties, the VCR (just now beginning to spread in the Soviet Union) the innovation of the seventies; next step—satellite TV. And who can tell what communications breakthroughs of the future will make ideological barriers even more fragile? Then, too, we may see the greatest breakthrough of them all: a period of liberalization that will allow émigré works to be published normally."

"The main advantage émigré authors have," said Cheryl, "is that they don't need to worry about being published 'normally' or writing for the drawer and the like; they're free to go their own way. As far as I can see, Socialist realism is synonymous with Soviet censorship."

"Yes, but what about the situation within the Soviet Union?" Melvin interrupted. "An article I read recently pointed out that the Soviet regime has nothing against good literature." General laughter. "It just needs to keep everything under control. If the literature that passes muster happens to be good, well, that's fine and dandy. Since even under Stalin a few decent works managed to make it into print, why not under Gorbachev or his successors? Besides, Russian history has had its share of surprises. As late as 1914 Lenin prophesied he wouldn't live to see the revolution. Is an outright revolt so out of the question? The supposed monolith is riddled with factions: technocrats, nationalists, the military. And even without a revolt there may come a time when the ruling oligarchy realizes that literature isn't a matter of life and death to the regime after all, that it can actually serve as a kind of safety valve."

"And don't forget," added Robert, "that even with ideological screws at their tightest, samizdat channels manage to hold their own. There's no going back to Stalinist times. Copy machines and word processors are under lock and key, but how long can a technologically oriented society keep them there? And what will become of repression when communication is as easy as pushing a button?"

On they went for three solid hours, these scions of the Mid-Atlantic States. And as they argued, I could feel it in the air. Yes, there it was. With a subject like ours it was only natural. Even the highly conditioned air of our American university was alive with the Russian metaphysical spirit!

All at once up jumped Matthew. "But repression is part and parcel of Russian literature. Without persecution, without suffering it will lose its freshness and originality, its traditional *moral* component."

"What shall we do with Matthew?" I asked the class. "Kick him out!" shouted some. "Give him another chance!" shouted others.

"Well, maybe I have gone a bit too far," Matthew admitted, "but it was Russian literature's moral stand that attracted me to it in the first place. And now that I think of it, Russian literature took that stand long before the Communists were in the picture: Russian literature has always dealt with internal, spiritual persecution and suffering. They are what gave Russian literature a place in world culture, a place it will surely regain in time."

Sketches for a Novel to Be

1985/ The HMN and his itinerant theater are playing a town in southern Virginia. The local intellectuals show him hills that 120 years earlier had seen battles between North and South. They get so heated up arguing about where the infantry advanced, when the cannons were brought in, and how the cavalries clashed that they completely forget about their guest.

"How many men fell in action?" the HMN asks somewhat condescendingly. But the figure he receives takes him aback. More than at Borodino!

They've certainly got a strange attitude toward their Civil War, he thinks. On the one hand, they talk about it as if it had been going on last year; on the other, they have no real rancor against the enemy and honor Northern and Southern heroes together. Over *there*, in our country (that is, in their country) it's just the oppostie. The Civil War is nearly as remote as Ivan the Terrible's campaign against Livonia, yet a Soviet city with monuments to the White Kolchak and Denikin side by side with the Red Frunze and Kotovsky boggles the imagination. Clearly, the Soviet chronogram is incompatible with the American magnetic needle.

14 I remember the night in August 1968 when, two years early, the sixties came to an abrupt end in the Soviet Union: Soviet troops had invaded Czechoslovakia.

In the ensuing weeks I followed *Pravda*'s coverage of events in both Prague and Chicago. According to the Prague correspondent, "Soviet troops have learned to recognize counterrevolutionaries by their appearance: jeans, stringy hair, mustaches, and beards—such are the distinguishing features of the enemies of socialism." His Chicago comrade, seething with the same righteous indignation, wrote: "The Chicago police brutally club the demonstrators. Anyone in jeans, anyone with a beard or long hair is fair game, for such are the sole distinguishing features of the 'disturbers of the peace.'" Clearly even *Pravda* discerned certain common denominators between East and West in those fatal years.

At the Kennan Institute I attended an interesting and convincing lecture about the similarities between the American radical thinkers of the 1960s and the Russian radical intelligentsia of the *186*0s. But I was more concerned with the parallels in our own day. As I see it, both American and Soviet culture emerged from the 1950s with a feeling that it was time to give up the sedative, hidebound isolationism of McCarthyism and Stalinism.

Not that I equate the two. As reprehensible as the senator's Un-American Activities Committee was, the number of people who fell victim to its machinations cannot compare with a single day in the operations of Stalin's "organs." What I have in mind is the feeling of sanctimonious righteousness that prevailed in both countries during the fifties and the moral, intellectual, and emotional experimentation that came to prevail, again in both countries and especially among the young, in the sixties.

It began in America with the beatniks, who, their Russian suffix -*nik* notwithstanding, could have no direct influence on Russian culture because no one was allowed to read them. But we did have bohemian enclaves where the values of the prerevolutionary avant-garde (in the persons of the futurists) held sway, and we did have the *stilyagi* I have described in connection with Russia's covert love affair with America. I have also mentioned the "youth prose" movement in our post-Stalinist literature and the euphoria we felt at being able to forge a language of our own and use it to treat real issues.

Still we could stage no sit-ins, no protest marches, no demonstrations of any kind. The Soviet counterpart of American overnight arrests would have been five- to ten-year stints in the camps, of American billy clubs and hoses—streams of lead. We did have one day of glory, however. In September 1974, after the famous Moscow Bulldozer Art Exhibition, when Komsomol crews under militia protection set fire to paintings by nonconformist artists and bulldozers moved on the crowd in true Stalinist fashion, the authorities felt the need for a concession and allowed an independent exhibition to take place on a field in Izmailovo Park usually reserved for training service dogs. It was a fine Indian summer day, and a crowd several thousand strong, representing Moscow's unofficial art colony, gathered to have a look at what was new in art and to show their solidarity with the daring artists. It was an unforgettable day and one never to be repeated (at least half of the artists, weary of senseless persecution, have since moved abroad, and probably a third of the art lovers have followed), but at least it gave us an inkling of what the "real" sixties had been like.

BREAD AND CIRCUSES

Not so long ago I had a chance to witness a live replay of those years in America. Maya and I were invited to attend a festival held annually in the hills of northern Vermont and called the Bread and Puppets Show, a hark back not only to the American sixties but also to the Roman bread and circuses tradition.

The majority of the crowd, which was several thousand strong and (if license plates are any indication) came from all over New England and beyond, had a leftist intellectual look to it, and everything, my friends assured me, was reminiscent of the late sixties: jeans, long hair, buttons, guitars, uninhibited dogs (our Ushik had a grand old time), and even more uninhibited babies (who crawled around naked in the heat). Every so often a knight-errant wandered over and helped himself to our jug wine, bestowing a vague but benign smile upon us all through the undergrowth on his face. Bread—tasty, homemade, whole grain—was handed out to one and all free of charge; it was, we were told, part of the tradition.

The first such festival dates back to the juncture of the sixties and seventies, when a German puppeteer by the name of Peter Schumann settled in Vermont. Since then his Bread and Puppets theater company has gained international fame. But after touring Europe, Latin America, and India, they always return to their natural amphitheater, the green hills of Glover, Vermont, about twenty miles from the Quebec border.

As we arrived on the scene and saw the rolling meadows, the tasseled flags, the colorful crowd, we might have thought we were about to attend a reenactment of the Wars of the Roses. In fact, what awaited us was quite the opposite: Bread and Puppets specializes in large-scale pacifist demonstrations and works closely with organizations like Grass Roots and Green World.

The program opened with pure, ideology-free pageantry: a Roman circus complete with emperor, patricians, gladiators, slaves, and wild animals; tumbling, singing, and comic speeches. The meadow has splendid natural acoustics, and every word resounded clearly across an enormous expanse.

As the sun started sinking, the antiwar action took over. Out from the trees filed a group of people clad all in white and holding a three-story-high puppet symbolizing the sun—and therefore peace. Then on a hill, a band of musicians appeared and filled the air with music. Finally, along a dirt path came a procession carrying a huge connubial bed with a three-story grandma and grandpa in it. Eventually they were joined by a kettle the size of a hut, and grandma set to making soup out of human potatoes, onions, peppers, parsnips, leeks, and tomatoes. All at once a stylized, robot-manned fighter plane, the monster of the fairy tale, zoomed out of the woods.

The villainy took place just as the sun sank behind the hills. But immediately a flock of doves appeared. One of them struck a match under the steel bird. Even as it turned into a bonfire, it continued to issue orders in a mechanical voice. By the time it had burned itself out, twilight had gathered and a majestic ark, the salvation of humanity, came floating overhead through a galaxy of ribbons, balloons, and glowing paper insects.

While the crowd drifted back to its cars, happy to have breathed some fresh air and participated in an antiwar ritual, our friends introduced us to one of the members of the company. He was very excited. "We're off to Europe soon to protest against the deployment of Pershings and cruises," he told us.

"Are you planning to protest against any other types of rocket?" we asked. "Soviet rockets, for example?"

At first he looked a bit confused, but he soon recovered and said, "The Russians have their own peace movement," he said. "I've seen pictures of meetings and marches."

We looked at his kind, trusting face and thought that his sort of idealism was indecent nowadays. By identifying the Soviet peace movement with his American one, he had fallen into the same trap as the naïve Soviets (the ones my students kept running up against) who assume that since repression exists at home it must also exist in America.

"Dear Nick," we told him, "feel free to consider the Soviet peace movement part of your Western peace movement: it too protests only against American rockets and nuclear warheads. And those marches and rallies you mention? Well, they're carefully staged and riddled with stoolies and undercover agents."

"You mean there is no independent pacifist movement in the Soviet Union?" he asked, astonished.

"What's the matter, Nick, old pal," we said, "haven't you ever read about the Moscow Group to Establish Trust? A few years ago a group of Muscovites tried to set up a peace organization of their own. They wanted to circumvent the official one, which is wholly subservient to the day-to-day requirements of Soviet propaganda, so they could do just what you do here: ask their government to wind down the arms race. And you know what happened to them? Fifteen ended up in psycho wards, several went to prison, several were forced to emigrate, and a few were 'allowed' to recant."

I think we got through to Nick, but what about all the others? The paradox is that without them America would not be America.

Sketches for a Novel to Be

1985/ The inexorable development of ethnic restauration can sometimes result in unheard-of monstrosities. Picture a French restaurant adorned with a mural of La Rochelle that features an overripe mermaid still wet from the waters. It's enough to give you second thoughts about Huguenot piety.

Then there's the neighboring gustatory palace, Nepalese style, where the laws of dialectical materialism come in for quite a beating, and in the language of its current perpetrators to boot. The proprietor, it turns out, spent five years at Patrice Lumumba University in Moscow. Then, instead of putting the progressive theories he had learned there into practice in his homeland, he decided to devote himself to the food business in the "citadel of capitalism." If the comrades only knew where their money was going.

But things get curiouser and curiouser. For the rest of the world Ethiopia is one big famine, but in Adams Morgan three Ethiopian restaurants have opened recently one after the other. And while Afghan mujahidin and Soviet helicopter pilots play hide-and-seek in the wilds of the Hindu Kush, in Bethesda's Kabul West, Soviet émigrés gather for genuine *shashlik*.

It all serves to bring people closer, as they used to say in Moscow, but it also means that good old Russian borscht is sometimes spoiled by German pepper.

15 We were driving up Interstate 95 from Florida, madly switching from one radio station to the next in the hope of avoiding the computerized mishmash of booming reggae and caterwauling rock, the endless commercials for mega-pizzas and macrobarbecues. The winter season was drawing to a close, and the entire highway would have looked like Connecticut Avenue at rush hour if all the cars hadn't been speeding along at sixty-five miles an hour. Constantly bombarded by the symbols of civilized provinciality—advertisements for gas, hamburgers, soft ice cream, and soft drinks—I suddenly felt an acute pang of nostalgia; suddenly I saw the old Moscow University, streets lined with snowbanks, the moon in a frosty haze, the end of youth, the beginnings of a new romance . . .

Why on the border of Florida and Georgia did I experience so palpable a feeling of Moscow? I wondered. And then I understood: the Jacksonville college station had invaded my radio with Gerry Mulligan's saxophone. Jazz, which in Russia had been the epitome of America to me, has now come to epitomize my Russian youth.

Now that I can swing into Georgetown anytime I please and drop in at Charlie's to hear Mel Tormé or move on a couple of hundred feet for a drink at Blues Alley, my knees practically bumping against the shoes of the legendary Woody Herman, I'm no longer amazed at superstars playing tiny joints. But during my first years in America I was shocked to learn that jazz was a rare guest in its homeland.

For my generation of Russians it was the voice of America soaring over the iron curtain on the airwaves of the Voice of America.

Why did we love it so? Perhaps for the same reason the Communists (and Nazis before them) hated it. For its refusal to be pinned down, its improvisatory nature. Living as we did in a totalitarian society, we needed relief from the structures of our minutely controlled everyday lives, of the five-year plans, of historical materialism. Traveling to Europe, especially to Eastern Europe, jazz became more than music; it took on an ideology or, rather, an anti-ideology. Jazz was a platonic rendezvous with freedom.

The first bebop copped from Willis Conover's Voice of America jazz beat program made its way across Russia in the form of homemade records cut on X-ray plates. Picture a group of Soviet adolescents in the early fifties standing openmouthed around a record player while an X-ray plate spins on the turntable at 78 revolutions per minute. For years Gillespie's horn and Goodman's clarinet passed through broken rib cages, inflamed bronchial tubes, and alveoli damaged by the silicosis of socialism. The underground industry that manufactured the disks was nicknamed Jazz on Bones.

It was only a matter of time before we Russians started playing jazz ourselves—first for school dances and fourth-rate clubs, later at full-fledged concerts. In the early days outraged Komsomol volunteers would start fights wherever jazz was played, but in time their leaders realized they would do better to co-opt it. They even took to sponsoring jazz concerts of their own—on the condition that the musicians steered clear of American songs and developed a purely Russian jazz (although jazz without American melodies is like a troika without horses).

The image of the Russian jazz musician has traveled from book to book in my works. The devotion of those men to their art! With no hope for money or fame they played whenever and wherever they could. When times were bad, they went underground—literally, like the early Christians—playing in boiler rooms and basements, leaving when chased out and appearing without fail when sent for. They cut themselves off from the main, "healthy" branch of society and even developed a language of their own. What can you do? their not particularly expressive faces and bent torsos seemed to say. Some of them grew old before their time; others stayed young all their lives.

Here are some excerpts from my Russian jazz prose:

1970/ I looked around and saw two or three hundred familiar faces, jazz musicians and their girls. Everyone had aged a bit, but some were even better-looking than before . . . They all played both hot and cool that evening, as if the dead drummer, the reason for the wake, were still with us and the whole thing were just one fantastic jam . . . There were times you felt like screaming, "Sit down, everybody! Can't you stop knocking, rustling, clicking, clucking, laughing, and blowing your noses? Give the musicians a chance to play. Life is short, and music is terrific!"

1969/ A bloodcurdling howl came through the half-open windows—Silvester playing on his baritone. He drowned out everything, even applause. When he blows into that curved horn of his, he's like an unclean spirit. Jazz has taken over his life . . .

"You ought to be ashamed of yourself, playing that stuff! It's not jazz, it's not even music. The authorities are right: you can't let 'Russian boys' into anything—not jazz, not literature. All they do is howl out their spleen, cough up their lungs, and take the razz out of jazz."

1 9 7 7 /   One warm May evening on the terrace of the Nabokov, Anton Luchnikov got the urge to serenade his pregnant wife. "Hey, J.J.," he said to one of the musicians, "let me have your horn for one number, okay?"

As he played, Anton looked straight at his wife, his eyes brimming over with love . . . "Well, how did you like it, sweetheart?" He smiled.

"Pretty good." She smiled back. "I always thought the saxophone was all talk with you, but you really can blow that thing after all . . . I'm going to write home tomorrow to tell Mom I was wrong: I thought I was marrying the next prime minister, and I married a sax player."

"Who gives a fuck about prime ministers?" mumbled Anton, embarrassed. "Jazz is a free and independent country. It doesn't need any of that politics crap."

1 9 6 3 /   "The builders of communism don't need jazz; they don't need all that crap. They need songs, romance!"

"That's wrong, comrade! That's a mistake! Jazz *can* help them! Jazz *is* romance! I bet that my clarinet here can make you fall in love with jazz in two hours."

"Have this comrade's documents checked!"

It must be difficult for Americans to appreciate the scope of this literally outlandish obsession. Why *should* "Russian boys" be so passionately attached to the music of so distant a country? Perhaps the very distance is what explains it. The inaccessibility. The Westernizing tendency among nineteenth-century Russians went only so far as Western Europe; their twentieth-century descendants carried it beyond the horizon. America has taken on all the overtones and syncopations of the West, and its music gives the Russian dreamer a new look.

MOSCOW INSULTS

Oscar Peterson and his trio came to Moscow in the mid-seventies. They were met at the airport by a bevy of bureaucrats from the State Concert Commission, people who had no idea who Peterson was and probably mistook the four of them for yet another black delegation. Black, as we have determined, meant progressive, and progressive meant you didn't need to stand on ceremony. As a result they were taken to a fleabag called the Urals. When Peterson demanded a hotel commensurate with his talent, the bureaucrats only laughed, and when the following day they refused to let him rehearse in the hall where he would be performing, when they showed him to a piano that was barely upright after all the hopaks and such pounded into it over the years, and when they told him there would be no press and no television, he said to his men, "Come on, let's get out of here," and off they went without a word to anyone—destination London and Ronnie Scott—and with a firm resolve never to set foot again in slushy, stuffy Moscow.

Was Peterson justified in going off in a huff or was he too easily miffed? Had he suffered some racial offense? (Blacks often feel uncomfortable in Moscow.) I don't think he would have left so easily if he had had any idea of what would happen that evening.

For that evening several thousand people gathered at the theater where he was scheduled to perform. A third of them, at best, had tickets; the rest had come to "commune." Many had flown in from outlying cities, from Siberia and the Caucasus, prepared to pay hefty premiums to scalpers hanging around the entrance.

Suddenly a rumor whipped through the crowd: the concert was off! The first thought was naturally that it had been banned. *They* never let *us* listen to jazz. I'll never forget the massive figure of a pianist famous in our jazz circles hulking sullenly on the theater steps, a cheap cigarette clamped between his teeth. He had been known as the "Moscow Peterson" all his adult life; he even looked like his prototype. Perhaps because he had a face accustomed to disappointment, he was able to hide his frustration at losing all hope of seeing and hearing Him in person. "Don't tell me you're surprised! What do you think they use for brains? You really don't know, do you?"

When someone overheard me say that I'd been to a Peterson concert in London a few years earlier, I was soon surrounded by a sea of faces all asking questions at once. The audience? Not many young people, basically forty and over. A third of the seats were empty. Did you hear that? A third of the seats were empty! What did he play? The classics, the golden oldies. By the time they got down to names of the trio, I was lost. Then I remembered that Peterson had brought on an old sax player and said he was a surprise. But I couldn't even recall whether he was black or white. "No, wait, he had a gray goatee. Yes, that's it!" "Coleman Hawkins! How could you forget Coleman Hawkins! Hey, this comrade here, he's heard Peterson and Hawkins *live.*" I felt embarrassed, as if I had just pinched something from the Jazz Hall of Fame. But the crowd looked on with genuine delight or, as they say in the Soviet Union, "good envy." No one seemed to know I was a fairly well-known writer; I was just the comrade who had heard Peterson and Hawkins *live.* A provincial intellectual standing next to me took off his cap, wiped the sweat from his face with it, and said, "Thanks for the story, comrade. At least I didn't make the trip for nothing."

The crowd on the Bersenevskaya Embankment was so caught up in its intoxicating disappointment that it did not disperse for several hours, the Kremlin towers staring across the river at it like a line of dispassionate guards.

A GENERAL'S ILLICIT PASSION

A few months before I left the Soviet Union, I ran into Genka Kvarkin in the underpass below Manège Square in Moscow. He invited me to his place. I was pretty much persona non grata by then, and not all my friends would have risked having me over, but he was a Soviet general with stars of authority on his shoulders. Besides, if he had heard anything about my nefarious affairs, it would only have been peripherally: he had been a jazz maniac all his life, and there was no room for extraneous sounds in his ears.

While we were students, we worked together for Jazz on Bones. We exchanged X rays and the latest news we had picked up from the Voice of America and Radio Monte Carlo. Even after the X-ray period was history and people started recording jazz on tape from contraband Western LP's, we continued to meet, and as the stars on Genka's epaulets increased, so did his jazz erudition. Once he read me some jazz poetry "written by a friend," but I wouldn't rule out Genka as the author. One of the poems opened like this:

> *Old Satchmo's blowing on his horn;*
> *The kids are in the yard.*
> *A man who knows what fate has in store*
> *Must find life pretty hard . . .*

Another had these lines:

> *But someone went and told Miles Davis*
> *That no one in the crowded hall*
> *Would dig his cadences at all.*
> *And he, unnerved and agitated,*
> *Combed the score all night in pain*
> *To find an error—but in vain.*

I wonder whether his superiors knew of this passion in a member of the strategic air command, which after all exists primarily to bomb the land of jazz out of existence. By the way, he had a worthy predecessor, the amazing Captain Kolbasyev of the prewar Baltic Fleet, whose jazz collection was the envy of many a jazzman (one of whom wrote a "Mokhovaya Street Blues" for him) and who was arrested and shot for his passion during the 1937 purges.

Times are different now, and Genka had a new apartment, special military rations (thick steaks), and a quadrophonic sound system. He played a triumphant parade of the Kings and Dukes of American jazz for us (a collection of that caliber could only have come from a pack of black marketeers—they haven't started stocking them at the Soviet equivalent of the PX) at excruciatingly high decibel levels (he was a military pilot, so they didn't bother him). All dinnertime small talk was out of the question. When we asked Madame Kvarkina how she coped, she mutely removed a pair of specially made earplugs. The general no more than picked at his steak; his eyes were elsewhere, ecstatic. When during one pause Maya heaved an ambiguous sigh, he hastened to reassure her that he still had some Johnny Hodges for her to listen to—oh, and a few cuts of Cannonball Adderley . . .

On our way down to the car he asked, "Well?"

"Great," I said. "By the way, we're off for the States pretty soon. We'll be hearing them all live."

He looked over at me and then up beyond the flat Moscow roofs, where a series of elongated, crocodile clouds stretched across the evening sky.

"It's not the same," he said, not the slightest bit jealous. "I don't go to their concerts when they come. You see, I don't want them to turn into living people, people like me. It would destroy my world. I need them to be inaccessible, I need their music to come from east of the sun and west of the moon . . ."

.   .   .

Even though jazz is still alive in America, it has been shunted off to a corner by the gigantic rock market. Rock has adapted wholeheartedly to the unwashed jerk-off set. Just as Elvis Presley gave up his leather jacket for the silly getup of an African-Marxist kinglet, today's big-buck rock has betrayed the swing aesthetic of the Beatles, decking itself out in spangles, beauty marks, gloves, and ruffles and attracting endless streams of square-assed, pimple-faced, scratchy-voiced, heavy-footed mediocrities who—worst of all—have no sense of humor whatsoever and try to make up for the lack by poking their fingers into the faces of their stoned audiences and abusing them with a string of lewdities.

Jazz, on the other hand, has never given in to the plebes and their bad taste. It is doing quite well in its own little corner, where we refugees from the East bloc venerate it as a part of our East-bloc nostalgia.

Sketches for a Novel to Be

1 9 9 0 / Nostalgia pains. Of all the orbital staff up at America Space, Mr. Flitflint had the reputation of being the least sentimental, and even he broke down and sobbed when earthling Slava Rostropovich flew in for a concert. But the moment the famous cellist left off sawing away at Beethoven, Flitflint went up to him and said, "Say, you wouldn't happen to know 'Melancholy Baby,' would you?"

16 When I look back on *Non-Stop Round the Clock,* the book of American sketches I wrote after a two-month stay in America in 1975, I am amused to note that they contain almost no criticism of American life. That spring in California must have been the most carefree period in my life. Twice a week I gave a seminar in my native language, and then off to Santa Monica Beach and days of hanging around, hanging out, hanging loose. Perhaps the California life-style is to blame for the carnivallike, hedonistic character of the book, though perhaps there was something more serious at work. Perhaps I used the sketches to shed the stereotypes of years of anti-American propaganda and Socialist realism. I saved all my criticism for my own country, with the result that five years later my own country threw me out.

Now I am completing my second book on America and am almost an American myself. I am accustomed to things that once irritated me: weak coffee, the smell of popcorn in move theaters; I am accustomed to putting the month before the day of the month, shouting "ouch" instead of "oy," and shaking my right hand when I find something exorbitantly expensive. As an "almost American" I see more than the bright windows of my new home; I see its mildewed corners as well. I trust that if I point them out my *new* country won't throw me out.

Sometimes, however, I'm not so sure. I have been labeled a "Komsomol hippie" and accused of raking in good money for lambasting American mass culture. When in the

New York Times Magazine I expressed the hope that my criticisms would not be taken amiss, a reader responded as follows: "We won't throw Aksyonov out of our country, but we will respond with a harsher retribution to his gloomy thoughts about our cultural life: we will ignore them!" What if my indignant reader suddenly relents and retreats to the position he considers less harsh? Where will we turn then? Where will we sail? America is the last frontier, isn't it? It's here or nowhere . . .

Non-Stop Round the Clock came out in the Soviet Union at the height of détente; it dropped in warm drops onto the bald pates of government officials while a hammer-and-sickle spaceship and a stars-and-stripes spaceship hooked up in space and, contrary to all expectation, Colonel Leonov did not ask for political asylum. In postdétente Moscow, books like the one I wrote, books with a positive message about America, cannot be published. The idea of the American way of life as an alternative to Soviet socialism drives the perpetrators of "historical progress" up the wall.

In Chapter Eight I cited a book of the kind that has taken its place (a book that has recently received the State Prize of the USSR), *The Face of Hatred* by Vitaly Korotich. Let me go into it in a bit more detail. The face of the United States, writes Korotich, is the face of hatred, hatred above all for the great Soviet Union, for its Communist ideology, for the world of socialism in general, in fact, for everything progressive, nonwhite, national-liberational, unionized, unemployed, young, hungry, impoverished, and peace-loving. The primitive nature of the lie seems to have satisfied those who commissioned it: it won't confuse anyone who has been reading the Soviet press for the past ten years.

The same idea, though in more sophisticated packaging, crops up among the literary ruminations of a particular group of intellectuals unofficially known as the National Bolsheviks—Natsbols, for short. The term is a self-contradiction of sorts, because the original Bolsheviks claimed to be *inter*nationalists. The Natsbols combine Russian chauvinism with hard-line totalitarian tactics. Following the time-honored Russian tradition, they use works of literature as springboards for philosophizing.

Stanislav Kunyaev, foe of cosmopolitanism and poet, scrutinizes the pages of Soviet poetry for the tiniest bedbug of pro-American feeling. He is especially attentive to that dangerous "abstract humanist" Andrei Voznesensky. When Voznesensky included the line "Two countries, two heavy hands intended for love" in a recent poem, Natsbol Kunyaev accused him of giving equal abstract-humanist weight to the Soviet system and a system "epitomizing the cult of violence and terror in today's world." Two such hands cannot come together in love, Kunyaev feels, thereby condemning the planet to one-handed love. Brrr! Even at its best, Kunyaev continues, America has cultivated violence instead of love: look at what it did to its indigenous population (as if the Russians had not conquered Siberia, central Asia, the Caucasus, and most recently the Baltic countries; as if the partitions of Poland were simply an extension of Russia's soothing hand).

Another Natsbol poet, Igor Shklyarevsky, has conscience enough to include in a recent antiwar poem a few kind words for the food America supplied the starving Soviets during the war (usually it is dismissed summarily: "We did the fighting; you sent the Spam"), but he goes on:

> *America, you are rich:*
> *You did not use women to plow,*
> *You did not wage war at home,*
> *You cannot measure our grief with yours.*
> *Today you have everything, but*
> *I wish you one thing more:*
> *Imagination.*
> *We shall cease to exist,*
> *But so will you.*

The Natsbols seem to think that America's riches descend from the heavens and have nothing to do with the energy of the people, the enterprise of the industrialists, and the desire of the entire population to build a strong, democratic, liberal society; they think that when the "riches" were handed out Russia was cheated and America profited from the deal. Having declared the plunder and ruin of their country the "greatest event in the history of man," having choked off democracy at its inception, having blindly obeyed the most arbitrary authority and accepted the most inefficient economic system, they fail to ask themselves, "Why did we need to use women to plow? Why were we forced to wage war at home?" Instead, they bark through the fence at their rich neighbor.

According to the Natsbol classification system (Marxism is so obsessed with classification I sometimes feel that if allowed to classify everything it would leave humanity alone), American culture consists of two main groups, the cosmopolitans and the nationals. Where Natsbol sympathies lie is not hard to guess.

For the critic Yury Seleznev, America's national writers are William Faulkner, Robert Frost, Erskine Caldwell, John Steinbeck, Robert Penn Warren, Thornton Wilder, and John Gardner. His colleague, Pyotr Palievsky, a leading theoretician, considers Faulkner an American Mikhail Sholokhov—though a second-rate Sholokhov, because while Sholokhov had gone beyond nineteenth-century humanism, all Faulkner had to offer was "the old human values." Still, Faulkner was important as a representative of "the sticks," the folk, as opposed to avant-garde cosmopolitans like, say, Joyce. Cosmopolitans against Russia, cosmopolitans against America, cosmopolitans against the world, cosmopolitans against life itself—such is the essence of the modern predicament Natsbol style.

Another shining light of National Bolshevism, Vadim Kozhinov, juxtaposes the forces of a "healthy renaissance" in American literature to "the dark forces of decay." He defines the latter as "postmodernists," in which category he includes Allen Ginsberg, Jack Kerouac, Lawrence Ferlinghetti, Kurt Vonnegut, J. D. Salinger, John Updike, Philip Roth, Norman Mailer, Jerry Rubin, Gerald Dworkin, Paul Goodman, Denise Levertov, and Karl Shapiro. The percentage cosmopolitan (that is, Jewish) names is always high on Natsbol lists of "dark forces," and the fact that many of the writers on Kozhinov's list were published in the Soviet Union in the sixties and seventies leads him to posit a world cosmopolitan conspiracy: the people responsible for putting them in print merely pretended to be acting in the interests of the Soviet Union; in fact, they were disseminating the works of writers whose goal was to undermine the Socialist way of life. For has not Reagan used the postmodern rebellion as a weapon of world imperialism and the CIA to further his vicious policies?

Moving on to the neoconservatives, among whom he lists Norman Podhoretz, Irving Kristol, Robert Alter, Charles Frankel, David Riesman, and Nathan Glazer, Natsbol Kozhinov runs up against a problem: the cosmopolitan ring of the names gets the Natsbol adrenaline going, yet the men behind the names are America's true "nationalists," to use the Natsbol terminology. Kozhinov handles the problem by decreeing that both groups (or "stages," as he calls them) are in complete harmony. "The aim of both stages is the same: to turn the American people into the obedient weapon of international imperialism and Zionism."

The final word, "Zionism," is of course the most telling. What the Natsbols really mean is "Down with the Jews! Up with both Russia and America!" The implication is that once the Jews are out of the way minor differences in ideology (like communism versus capitalism) will take care of themselves. Oddly enough, Kozhinov's ignorant ravings show the first glimmerings of an appeal to America, the "healthy forces" of America, that is. All those healthy forces have to do is to throw off the "old human values" and the two sides can sit down and talk.

· · ·

Ignorance, prejudice, and mythmaking are unfortunately not limited to the National Bolsheviks. Soviet officials on all levels are also guilty. What is worse, they come to believe the false stereotypes they create for themselves.

It is fashionable now, especially since the fall of Saigon, to look down on America. Once upon a time America was a benchmark: Lenin called upon Russia to combine "the Russian revolutionary spirit with American business sense," and Khrushchev kept promising to "catch up with and surpass America." The current tendency is to talk about America with a sardonic grin.

I happened to be at a Baltic writers' resort when a favorite of the regime, just back from America, swaggered on the scene. The comrade's belly hung down over his stiff new Levi's; his Polaroid hung down over the belly. Before dinner he kept snapping pictures of his totally Americanized family, smugly holding up the results (most people present had never seen a Polaroid camera before); after dinner, over cognac, he carried on about America's "false orientation" (a pouting lower lip) and "feeble guts" (a snigger) and summed it all up by calling the country (in English) "misleading and misled."

Another highly characteristic (and highly dangerous) trait of National Bolshevism is its disdain for the strength of America and the West in general. As far as the Natsbols are concerned, Europe presents no problem: we'll blow it away if we have to.

The new Natsbol messiah, the poet Yury Kuznetsov, has a frankly Nazi view of Europe. He would have the youth of Russia saddle up their horses and "gallop to France, a city [*sic*] on the ruins of great ideas." Nor does he see any military or moral impediments: "We don't care what the descendants of its once gilded, now faded population will say . . . The only memory that matters to me is Russian memory! . . . No one will weep over sacred foreign stones but us."

Here we have the Natsbol dream in all its glory. But Kuznetsov had better think twice about his horses. If his horsemen so much as ride up to the gates of France-City, they'll be hit so hard they won't be able to count their hoofs. National Bolshevism may be vicious, but it is also congenitally craven. It knows the answers before the facts, relies on a selective, ideologically tinged memory, and has no concept of the modern world, European military strength, or, for that matter, the thoughts of several million dissident Russians.

A widespread myth among the Natsbols has it that "Americans are poor soldiers," that they are pampered and decadent. (As for their perception of the American intellectual, I would venture to say that it coincides with the perceptions of the denizens of American stadiums and bars, the rednecks and tough guys who form the backbone of the country.) But Americans don't like to lose. The American boys in Vietnam never lost a battle. What happened was that the war turned into a battlefield for various home-baked points of view. Soviet apparatchiks have no reason to feel superior: whenever their drones bearing regulation-issue ideas of "the most progressive of societies" set off in the direction of America, they always fly splat up against it.

Perhaps most basic to this "new disdain" is a contempt for America's lack of unity: Soviet society is unified, American society fragmented and therefore weak. What the Soviets cannot fathom is that America's "fragmentation" (in other words, its diversity) is the source of its magnetic strength. If America was unified along Soviet or Iranian lines, it would no longer be America. It must therefore instill in its population a passionate desire to defend its multiplicity, its ferment, its intellectual and aesthetic waverings, its hedonism, its morality, its ecumenism, its ethnic variety, its Anglo-Saxon foundations, its generosity, its technology, its elemental counterrevolutionary spirit, its hope for a new liberal era, and all its capitalists, tramps, superstars, farmers, union members, journalists, politicians, feminists, priests, ministers, homosexuals, lesbians, sectarians, fortune-tellers, postmodernists, wrestlers, street musicians, gamblers, refugees, punks, models, filmmakers, stockbrokers, go-go girls, tax inspectors, yes, even its real estate agents . . .

Let me call a spade a spade: the anti-Americans of this world—Gabriel García Márquez included—are enemies of freedom and friends of a global concentration camp. The paradox of it all is that to remain what it is America must defend even its own anti-Americans.

It is raining in Georgetown. Everything is in slow motion. Cars float toward one another in the rhythm of a leisurely rainfall. We inch along elegiacally in our Baby Benz past houses with brass doorknobs and picture windows with comfortable-looking fireplaces, past figurines of ducks and flamingos, past ethnic restaurants and shops displaying the latest in footwear, tobacco, furniture, in elegance and extravagance, and then, rising slightly, we cross a canal that still has its wooden sluices, and at the end of the street we make out a gray strip of the Potomac and a blurry red traffic light half blocked by patches of raincoats and wedges of multicolored umbrellas and by the laughing faces walking past. "Ah, American rain," says a friend visiting from Moscow.

A few days earlier we had bumped into her at the Lincoln Memorial. Maya turned to me and said, "Look at that woman sitting on the steps. Doesn't she look like Galya Gruzdevaya?"

During the first few years after we emigrated, familiar Moscow faces kept popping up everywhere. A senator in the papers looked just like Zhenka, a bartender like Vitka, a bank teller like Irka, and so on. Even the basketball players on television reminded us of Zhorkas, Tankas, Svetkas, and Mishkas.

But this time Galya Gruzdevaya's double stood up and turned into Galya Gruzdevaya. The comrades had finally let her attend a scientific congress in America. No, she hadn't tried to phone; she didn't have the number. Oh, she could have found it out in Moscow, but she was afraid: a visa had to be treated like porcelain. What if they learned she was friends with Aksyonov?

"And now we meet. I was just thinking about you, and here you are. No, no. I'm not afraid now: I'm in America."

We're on our way to Georgetown for dinner. She stares out of the window beyond the splashes of rain, until I spy a spry young man going up to his Camaro. I roll down the window and ask, "Are you leaving?" He smiles: "You're in luck."

"How odd it is to hear you speak English," says Galya.

"It's an odd way of life," we agree. "Alone, we speak Russian, but roll down a window, and the whole world changes."

"You know," Galya muses as she looks around at the perfectly ordinary collection of people in the Chinese restaurant, "I sometimes think it's a lot harder for Americans to die than it is for us."

"You mean you think there's no grief here?" Galya is a biologist and no longer young, and like all Soviet women biologists of a certain age she is fundamentally tired.

"No, and no less drama, but less depression, humiliation. Less wasting away. Life is more human here; it's harder to leave than the life we lead."

"But it's the only life they know. Completely ordinary. They can't begin to imagine the life you so metaphorically call 'ours.' "

One April afternoon I am out walking Ushik in Rock Creek Park. Although there are embassies ten minutes away, everything here is wild and woodsy. A brook, a path, a few slopes, and cherry trees, oaks, chestnuts, maples. We are alone. Ushik is busily looking for something among the rocks, tossing aside last year's leaves with his hind legs.

Everything is motionless in the diffuse gray light. I stand transfixed by the steep, flowering slope of neighboring Dumbarton Oaks, by the pinks mixed with patches of bright yellow and wisps of white against the gentlest of greens, and suddenly I am certain that I am gazing on the soul of my recently departed ninety-two-year-old Aunt Xenia. She had died in Kazan six months before, but the news took five months to reach me. Letters from Kazan rarely made their way to Washington, and a phone call from Washington would have brought out the entire local KGB contingent.

Aunt Xenia, my father's sister, did not come up to his shoulder and had a potato nose and wonderful blue eyes. Her husband died back in World War I, and she had been alone ever since—not counting the hordes of children, generation after generation, she was called upon to bring up.

I entered her household in Kazan at the age of five after my parents had been arrested in the purges. I stayed with her until I was sixteen, when I went off to Magadan and exile with my mother. During the war, when only women and children were left in Kazan, Aunt Xenia would go out to the local flea market, rain or shine, and hawk other people's wares for a percentage of the profit. We children would wait by the window for her to return and bring us a chunk of bread, some onions, or a couple of kilograms of potatoes. Sometimes, her thin lips pressed together, she would make her way home through a storm with nothing. But every evening she would chop the knotty wood—oh, how her sighs made us suffer—and round up something for the pot.

Once in a great while she would also wash us. I remember myself standing in the washtub. She is scrubbing a disgustingly filthy foot with a mop. Suddenly she steps back, as if to admire the results of her labor, and says, "Well, compare this one with that. Which do you like better?" We both laugh. A happy moment. My aunt loves me!

When she was alive, people always said she had a big

heart. Meeting her on that flowering slope, I saw what a peaceful, tranquil beauty she must have been.

The Bolsheviks threw me out of my native country, cut me off from family graves, but souls still fly about without their permission and appear to exiles in the vapors above the American soil.

Sketches for a Novel to Be

1985/ (From the HMN's diary.) Suddenly I realize I'm lying on a bed so hard that it makes me think of *that* life. The unpleasant associations are heightened by a stain on the wall strangely resembling the one that appeared *there* in 1969, when Victoria threw a jar of mayonnaise at me but missed, after which all I had to do was look at the stain meaningfully for her to stop arguing and leave the room.

Luckily, these are just the whims of my unconscious. The sun is pouring through the Beethoven Street window with its usual intensity. It's one of those mornings, not so unusual *here,* when the world seems to have changed for the better overnight—or at least not to have changed for the worse: nobody blown up, nobody kidnaped.

Then a chill, akin to a hangover spasm, goes through me, and I start wondering if I've been kidnaped myself. In the distance—though perfectly clearly—I hear someone saying, "The harvest is proceeding at record speed. The toilers in the fields have taken Comrade Gorbachev's remarks to heart."

As usual I turn on the TV with the big toe of my left foot. I feel a surge of relief: it's good old Bryant Gumbel on the screen. True, he says *Dobroe utro* in perfect Russian, but only because NBC is broadcasting live from Moscow and *our* newscaster has picked up a few words of *their* lingo.

I have neither coffee nor beer in the kitchen to "fix my head." I'm taken aback once more: another expression from *over there*. I haven't had a hangover here in ages.

I head for the 7-Eleven. Beethoven Street looks weird. The Filipino who usually sells hotdogs and ice cream (his whole business depends on people too lazy to walk the hundred yards to the 7-Eleven) has been replaced by a well-dressed Uzbek with a gold Choibolsan medal on the lapel of his artificial-fiber jacket. What's he doing here? Oh, he must be one of the members of the visiting "parliament" delegation at the Hilton. Looking for a whore, I bet . . .

But what if? I break out in a sweat and rush into the store, my heart pounding like a horse's. I grab the latest *Penthouse* from the stand, leering at the thought of what horses, whose thighs, will adorn the cover? In the mirror I see a horse's head, in my hand a copy of *Soviet Screen.* The following editorial leaps to my eyes: "Is there a person in our country today who is not pondering how he measures up to the decisions of the April plenary session of the Central Committee of the Soviet Communist Party?"

What has happened? Have they transported me overnight from *our* city to *theirs,* I mean, to our *over there* from their *over here,* in other words, to this past from that present?

Things are still moving, swirling, winking, beckoning to me. There are still all kinds of things for sale. But I feel unsteady. Like a criminal.

A taxi! If there's the slightest chance to hold on, I must find it. I have plenty of taxis to choose from: Yellow Cab, Atlantic, Five Star, Blue Top . . . But for some reason I choose an olive one with no lettering, only a few squares from a checkerboard. "Step on it," I tell the driver, who immediately launches into a lusty harangue against the government: "Bastards, vipers, sweep them out with a filthy

broom!" "If you don't like the government," I tell him,
"vote in a new one!" "Got any Solzhenitsyn, pal?" he asks,
his gypsy eyes sparkling. You won't catch me, I think. I
know an agent provocateur when I see one. I start singing
something like "Those Fabulous Flights," but out comes
the nauseating "We Are the Red Cavalry." The cab stops
at the Union of Creative Unions. I see guards with the
fourth and second letters of the Russian alphabet, G and
B, on their epaulets. "Where have you brought me, you
asshole?" I ask. "This is the right address, isn't it?" the
slave replies with a sob. "Take me where I still have a
chance," I say. Where? Where have you still got a chance?
You haven't the slightest idea.

The square billows into a cobblestone mound and flat-
tens out along the edges, as if in a wide-angle lens—agora-
phobia surrounded by the claustrophobia of hulking
buildings, all brick and polished stone, all crenellations,
spires, goat-footed cornices, twisted-turban cupolas, all Socialist Byzantium.

An endless line stretches along the edge of the square
and flows into rectangular blackness. Although everyone is
supposed to be solemn, someone is chewing quietly, someone else, peeking up his sleeve, is reading a book. They
have no chance whatsoever, and still they don't waste time.
Or do they each nurture a last hope like me?

Around the corner of a building that looks like the coffer
of a Persian monarch comes the oval snout and sloping
forehead of a Boeing 747. This must be my chance—I *must*
get across the square. But I can't manage it alone: agora-
phobia will blow me away like a butterfly.

I finally tear myself away from the never-ending line and
stagger up to the top of a mound, where I sway in the wind.

Luckily, a crowd of airline passengers, some three hundred of them, appear in the tower gates and start walking toward me. They walk at a steady pace, their bags, cameras, and briefcases and an assortment of tennis rackets and golf clubs over their shoulders or in their hands. They are a motley group—some tanned and glowing (straight from Miami), others pale and harried (from nowhere but New York); some in casual attire and all but barefoot, others in country-club finery; some laughing mutely, intensely excited, as if just released from Beirut captivity, others brooding, as if thinking over a deal just made in Chicago.

Two or three portraits. A cute little, chubby little waitress in tight jeans and a T-shirt proclaiming I'M SEXY!—neither Crimea nor the Caucasus has seen the likes of that ass. A working millionaire in a long coat of Scandinavian furs gliding along—eyes on the ground, slightly embarrassed by his wealth—like a Rolls-Royce among Volkswagens. A trim woman executive with a stern expression on her face but a come-hither slit up her skirt. A long-armed, bug-eyed fellow wearing a Puma T-shirt with a picture of same and red hair bursting out all over.

My goal was to make my way over to these *fellow citizens* of mine, to move as far as I could from my *fellow countrymen,* who were staring out indifferently from the line at the agoraphobic landscape. Shakily, clumsily, I did my best to keep time with the airplane crowd, approaching them at an angle and trying not to attract the attention of the towers by walking too fast.

And before long I had in fact blended into the noiselessly marching, gesticulating, articulating crowd. I looked around in all directions, and I seemed to see a lot of friends or at least familiar faces: my condo neighbors, joggers, truck drivers, patrolmen, professors liberal and conservative, aging hippies, two poets and five filmmakers, D.C. diplomats, Chinese chefs, a director, an admiral, a woman writer of romantic bent, a lawyer and his clerk, Hopkins students and Amazon students, a couple of presidential candidates, football fans, feminist activists, beggars, yuppies, a photographer with three cats, robbers, a priest, a council of Russian specialists, jazzmen, a nudist, Jane Fonda, Frank Zappa, Romeo, Mercutio, the Nurse . . .

So my chance had worked, but if it had, why didn't the others on the other end of the square, the end with the crenellated shadows, try to join us, walk with us? Don't wait for an answer, I told myself.

The red-headed fellow in the Puma shirt—Mr. Flit-flint?—pursed his lips and started whistling a tune. At which point the sound came on.

Vermont, July 1984
Paris, July 1985

About the Author

VASSILY PAVLOVICH AKSYONOV, who is generally acknowledged as the leading Soviet writer of his generation, was born in Kazan in 1932. His father was a Communist party official. His mother, Eugenia Ginzburg, a historian, won international fame as the author of the memoirs *Journey into the Whirlwind* and *Within the Whirlwind,* in which she recounted her experiences of nearly two decades in Stalin's camps.

Aksyonov spent part of his childhood with his mother in exile in Magadan, Siberia, "farther from Moscow than from California," as he puts it, and his own re-creation of that experience can be found in the pages of *The Burn.* He was later educated as a doctor, graduating from the First Medical Institute of Leningrad in 1956. His first novel, *The Colleagues,* published in 1960, was followed in 1961 by *Half-way to the Moon,* which attracted the attention of the world press and established his reputation as the representative of a new, Western-oriented, questioning generation of Soviet youth.

Aksyonov's prodigious activity as a novelist, short-story writer, dramatist, and screenwriter soon earned him a place at the forefront of Soviet cultural life. Although frequent clashes with government authorities made it increasingly difficult for him to publish at home, he was one of a few writers permitted to travel abroad. In 1975 he was a visiting lecturer at the University of California at Los Angeles.

In 1979 he spearheaded the effort to create a literary anthology free of censorship, *Metropol,* and resigned from the Writers' Union after two of his fellow editors were expelled. Deprived of his citizenship during a stay in America, he now lives in Washington, D.C., with his wife, Maya. He has been a Fellow of the Kennan Institute for Advanced Russian Studies there and is currently teaching at Goucher College and at Johns Hopkins University in Maryland.

Aksyonov's work is now published throughout the Western world. A collection of short stories, *The Steel Bird and Other Stories,* appeared in English translation in 1979. His satiric fantasy, *The Island of Crimea,* received wide acclaim when it was published in 1983, as did his masterpiece, *The Burn,* when the English translation was published in 1984. A new novel—*Say Cheese*—is forthcoming.